What readers say

"… one of the best structured, most comprehensive and least biased books I have read about love …"

"I once read 'The Power of Now' and I think it is as life changing for myself & others to read that book, as it is to read yours.

I read your book in bed at night, and seriously there were times when I couldn't wait to go to bed, because I wanted to learn more. It taught me a lot about myself, and gave me an insight into what went wrong in former relationships.

What I liked most were the parts in which you gave examples of your own life and relationships. That made it easy to relate to, and helped me to feel that having 'challenges' in a relationship is really OK."

"… opened my mind to a new world …"

"I read your book last week, and I must say, it rocked me to the core. I realized how little of love I knew. I could've been your case study. I exhibited all the irrational behaviors and thought patterns you speak about.

Thank you for writing such a wonderful book. It has helped me a lot. I will highly recommend it to anyone I feel needs some direction."

"… your vision for transforming sexual bliss … is beautifully written, and is one of the best works of this kind I have read."

"… Frank Vilaasa shows us how to align brain, heart and soul to achieve higher levels of love … he is obviously dedicated to the higher principles of love in his life and work. The book gives clear, constructive checklists for how to recognize our illusions about love, and how to break free from stuck patterns.

Written for health professionals and for lay people, the advice on how to grow into a more loving person by practicing awareness, acceptance and affirmation will be easy for anyone to follow. It has inspired me in my work and my life …"

"… 'What is Love' touched my heart in a profound way… it is so good, I want to share it with my friends, so I am ordering more copies."

Other books by Frank Vilaasa

Understanding Holistic Health
– Your Complete Guide to Health and Wellbeing

FRANK VILAASA

WHAT IS LOVE?

The Spiritual Purpose of Relationships

Human publishing

Published by Human Publishing
Sankt Olsgade 10C, 4000 Roskilde, Denmark

Cover symbol by Daniel Mooij (www.portraitno1.com)
Illustrations: © Frank Vilaasa (page 24) and
© Sentha Dhakini (page 32)
Sri Chinmoy quote in Chapter 2
taken from www.yogaofsrichinmoy.com
Second edition, first printing

Printed and bound by CPI Group (UK) Ltd, Croydon, CR0 4YY

ISBN 978-87-988722-6-9

www.humanpublishing.com
info@humanpublishing.com

For Shakti

Acknowledgements

In developing my understanding of the ideas in this book, I have received guidance and inspiration from a number of sources. I would like to express my gratitude to the many teachers of Tibetan Buddhism, especially The Dalai Lama and Sri Dharmakirti. Also to Osho, Swami Nityananda, Barba Tulku Rinpoche, Wilhelm Reich, Gerda Boyeson and Dr J R Worsley.

Many people have helped with the preparation of this book. My special thanks are due to Sentha for her encouragement, support and comments, and to the following for their suggestions and feedback Eileen Meehan, Ninad, Shanti Shivani and Michael Ulrich.

'I have three treasures
The first of these is love'
– Lao Tzu, Tao Te Ching

Contents

====

Preface

===

This book is suitable for anyone who wishes to attain their full potential for sharing love with another. If love is missing from your life, you will find many useful guidelines here for how to make it manifest.

The book's subtitle is 'The spiritual purpose of relationships'. This reflects the fact that the quest for love is part of our spiritual journey. Whether we know it or not, we are all spiritual beings, and the spiritual journey consists in removing the barriers that prevent us from fully realizing this.

Traditionally, in the East, this inner journey was undertaken alone, or within a monastic community. The traditions of Tibetan Buddhism, Zen and Yoga have developed many different guidelines for the spiritual path. One thing they have in common, however, is a recognition of the importance of awakening the heart as part of this journey. It is through the heart that we connect directly with the deepest sense of ourselves – our divine nature. The heart is the doorway to the divine, and it is through awakening the heart that we access the deeper layers of our spiritual nature.

The traditional way of doing this was mostly through the cultivation of loving kindness and compassion, through devotional practices such as chanting, and through the guru-disciple relationship. Relationships between men and women were not an acceptable part of this process. Women were seen as a distraction to men on the spiritual path, and monks were generally forbidden to spend time in their company. Most Buddhist monks and Hindu yogis have traditionally practiced celibacy.

There seems to have been two main reasons for this. Firstly, in Eastern cultures, the demands of a family life conflicted with the demands of the spiritual quest. Women were often financially dependant on their husbands, and family life – for both men and women – was seen as too time consuming to allow the spiritual seeker to follow a spiritual practice.

Another more unspoken reason was that young monks and yogis were not considered mature enough to deal with the potentially addictive pleasures of sex. Without sufficient self-discipline, there was a danger they would give in to the temptation to indulge. Indulgence creates a low energy state, which is unsuitable for spiritual practice. Dealing with one's wandering mind in meditation was considered challenging enough, without having to handle the desires provoked by the presence of a female partner every time you stepped off the meditation cushion.

Within Eastern cultures, the celibate approach to spiritual life has worked reasonably well. Many in these traditions have attained to high levels of spiritual realisation. However, when teachers from Eastern cultures come to the West, they often show themselves to be naive and inexperienced in relating to women, and unable to handle the freedom of Western culture.

Within the traditional teachings there is almost no mention of how an intimate relationship can be part of the spiritual journey. Yet for many Westerners involved in spiritual practice, a relationship often continues to be a part of their life. This book has been written to bridge this gap between Western lifestyle and traditional teachings. Based on my own journey, my work with clients and students, and on teachings I have received from a variety of sources – both traditional and modern – these pages contain insights and guidelines for awakening the heart within a relationship.

There are several very good reasons why including a relationship as part of the spiritual journey is particularly suited to people from the West.

Firstly, Westerners generally have more difficulty being open-hearted than people form the East. Eastern cultures are more heart-centred, and for a Buddhist monk living in a monastic community, the sense of belonging and connectedness are still very strong. The loneliness that is prevalent in the West is far less so in the East. Hence for Westerners, the cultivation of love and open-heartedness is a more necessary and challenging requirement.

Secondly, we in the West are more sexually liberated. In traditional Eastern cultures, the only way to enter an intimate relationship was to get married. This brought with it all the responsibilities of providing for one's wife and family. In the West, many different forms of relationship are now acceptable, and women are generally not a financial burden on the man. Men and women now enjoy a far greater freedom and independence within a relationship and, for Westerners, an intimate relationship need not be a distraction on the spiritual path.*

Finally, there is the fact that, in Eastern cultures, the spiritual quest was undertaken mostly by men. In the West, there are at least as many women interested in spirituality as there are men. This creates the possibility for a couple to support each other in their practice, and to share the journey together.

For all these reasons, I believe that the spiritual journey – the enquiry into our true nature – is enhanced by what we discover about ourselves as a result of being with someone else. This is what makes the sincere search for love in a relationship such a powerful spiritual practice.

---

* Note regarding sexual orientation. The parts of this book dealing with sexuality are written from the perspective of a heterosexual relationship. The principles on which the book is based, however, are universal, and can be applied equally well to same-sex relationships.

Introduction

This book is about how you can bring more love into your life. It is a common, yet puzzling experience to see both our own and other people's relationships start to flounder after some time. We all enter our relationships with great hopes and the best of intentions – and yet we often find ourselves getting bogged down in arguments, disappointments, demands, possessiveness, boredom and other relationship pitfalls. The love that was there in the beginning so often gets trampled under by each person's frustrated expectations.

It's not that we can avoid these pitfalls. Everyone will experience their share of frustration, disappointment, possessiveness, anger and so on during the course of a relationship. This is part of our human nature. The problem is that no-one has ever shown us how to deal with these things effectively. Our way of dealing with difficulties often makes things worse. We refuse to take responsibility for our part of the story. We blame the other person. We rationalize our mistakes. We don't want to be seen as being in the wrong.

Many people approach love with unrealistic ideas and expectations. When difficulties arise in a relationship, your conditioning is to see them as problems. You think something is going wrong. So you start to wonder – whose fault is this? Who screwed up? Apart from yourself, there is only one other person in the room at that moment. It is quite clear – in your mind – that the difficulty really has nothing to do with you. Like an astute detective, through a process of elimination, you point your finger at the guilty party. It's an open and shut case. There's the culprit standing right in front of you!

To your dismay, the culprit refuses to take the blame. They get defensive. They even come back at you with some finger-pointing of their own.

You have entered the blame-game. This game can be played out in a heated, overt way – or in an unspoken, internalized way. Either way, it undermines the positive regard and trust necessary for a relationship to flourish.

In this book, we will look at how to deal with relationship difficulties effectively. We will see that difficulties are not a problem – they are actually one of the reasons why you have come together.

Why do we enter into a relationship with another person? On one level, we do so for companionship, mutual support and the sharing of life's joys and challenges. Yet there is a deeper reason that we don't often recognize. We are there to learn how to love. The reason we don't recognize this is that we imagine we already know how to love.

This idea that we already know how to love, is what causes most relationships to break down. It is the root cause of the blame-game. After all, if I already know how to love, how could I be in any way responsible for love disappearing? So we blame the other person for the difficulties in our relationship. And we remain blind to our share of the responsibility.

You will never learn something if you can't admit that right now you are not skilled at it. Of course, some forms of unskillfulness are easier to admit to than others. We don't mind admitting that we can't build a web-site. But admitting that we don't know how to love? That goes right to the core of who we are as human beings. Even admitting it to ourselves can be devastatingly humbling.

We spare ourselves this humiliation by recalling those times when we did experience and share love. It is true that most of us have known love at some time or other. Does this mean we have reached our full potential as lovers? Can we say that we are satisfied with what we have known? Is it enough? If you are honest with yourself, you will recognize that it is not. There is a longing in every human heart for a love that is on-going. And when we look at the reality of our situation right now, we see that this longing often remains unfulfilled.

This doesn't mean that you have to leave the relationship you are in. If there are difficulties in your relationship right now – that's perfect! This relationship can become your classroom, and the difficulties your homework assignments. It would be very helpful if your partner could join you in the classroom, but even if they are unwilling to, you can still take the opportunity to work on your own issues. Just you getting clearer within yourself will change the dynamics of the relationship.

You will find that once you have taken a couple of semesters, love starts to become more of a reality in your life. Love is not only for the lucky – it is for the honest and the sincere. It is for those who are willing to learn.

There is an assumption at the heart of this book. The assumption is – that relationships are meant to be challenging. This goes against the whole Hollywood/ fairytale/ romantic/ Mills & Boon mythology of relationships that we have been brought up with. We think relationships are about sharing a love that is openly and constantly flowing. And when things don't work out this way – something has gone wrong.

The reality is – nothing has gone wrong. We are in a relationship to experience those parts of ourselves that interfere with the free flow of love – and to transform them. We are there to learn. None of us is perfectly loving. As human beings, we are all on a journey to reach our full potential. And in a relationship, our full potential is to love openly and freely. In a relationship, we are each other's teachers and students. A teacher doesn't blame the student for making a mistake. A teacher is empathetic and encouraging. The teacher thinks 'How can I make this more clear?' That's how we should be with our partner when we see them being less than perfect. And when we make a mistake, we should be willing to admit it – at least to ourselves.

When these things are understood, amazing things will happen. The whole dynamic of your relationship will change. Rather than all the blaming and finger-pointing, there will be the excitement of mutual discovery and growth. You will support each other in reaching your full potential, taking delight in your breakthroughs and achievements along the way.

The questions for you will become 'What relationship curriculum do I want to follow?' and 'How can I best reach my full potential?'

In this book, a set of guidelines is given that covers almost every aspect of intimate relationships. Money, sexuality, possessiveness, jealousy, control, assertiveness, honesty, vulnerability, judgments, attachment are just some of the issues we will explore in detail. These are the main places where people get stuck. Love may be there – but possessiveness can stifle and destroy it. Excessive control or judgment can destroy it. Yet we will find that at some time or other, one or more of these issues will plague our relationship. If we can meet the challenge of dealing with an issue head-on, we can transform it. It will no longer be the stumbling block that causes our relationship to flounder.

This is one of the main purposes of relationships – to transform ourselves into loving beings. We won't discover our possessiveness or judgments out on the golf course, or sitting on a meditation cushion. We discover them in the nitty gritty of an intimate relationship. The message of this book is – this discovery is an essential part of reaching your full potential. How you can use this discovery for your own benefit is what this book is about.

In addition to learning how to transform and overcome your negative tendencies, we will also explore those qualities that will enhance your relationship. Maximizing sexual bliss, improving communication skills, developing trust and honesty, cultivating forgiveness and gratitude, balancing control with spontaneity are some of the positive qualities that, when you cultivate them, will greatly improve your relationship.

All of this takes time. We won't achieve these things overnight. However, on this journey, our joy comes not from reaching some goal, but from traveling the path. The discoveries and breakthroughs we make on the way, and the ever-deepening connection we feel evolving, are what make the journey worthwhile.

I still consider myself a learner on the path of love. I have not discovered an end point to it, although I have been traveling it for many years. At first, I was filled with romantic ideas about love. I believed that you fell in love, and the feeling would last forever. So I was surprised to discover my girlfriend having bad moods, and myself becoming disappointed in her. I was also surprised at our arguments, and the stubbornness with which both of us refused to yield. Bit by bit, my romantic illusions where swept aside by the reality of two people struggling with different aspects of their natures.

Since then I have been in several significant relationships. It was not until I met my first spiritual teacher that I started to explore the ups and downs of my relationships in a conscious way. I started to pay attention to my old habits of wanting to be in control. I discovered a possessive side to myself. I became aware of my judgments. At the same time, I started to notice what effect these things had on myself and on my partner. Whenever I was judging her, I noticed her getting defensive, and feeling offended. It didn't matter whether I was right or not, she was not willing to listen to me at that moment.

With the guidance of my spiritual teacher, I started to adjust my attitudes and behavior. I started to let go of the attempts at control. I learned to respect my partner's freedom, and at the same time, not allow my own freedom to be interfered with. I gave up 'trying' to create a loving connection, and learned to just let it happen. Over time, these and other lessons started to sink in – and my relationships changed dramatically. Gone were the hassles, the tension, and the insecurity. In their place a mutual positive regard arose – and a lot of love.

The ideas in this book have come, not from academic study, but from my own struggles to find love, and from my work as a counsellor, therapist and meditation teacher. Dealing with many different relationship issues with a wide variety of people has deepened my understanding of what works and what doesn't work in a relationship.

I have used the model of the seven chakras as a way of giving some order and clarity to the various difficulties we deal with in relationships. The Tantric Yoga chakra system mirrors very closely the most common issues that confront couples. Money, sexuality, jealousy, possessiveness, power and control, love and intimacy are the main issues we face in a relationship. They are also what the energies of the first four chakras are all about. The chakra system is explained in more detail in Chapter Two.

For the purposes of this book, which is to provide guidelines for finding love in an intimate relationship, we will follow the model of the chakras up till the fourth chakra. This is the heart centre, and is where the journey to find love comes to fulfillment.

It is my intention to follow this book with a second book to describe the journey of the last three chakras. In that book, we will look beyond the dynamics of a one-to-one relationship, to our connection with life and the universe. We will find that the skills we learn in an intimate relationship greatly improve our connection to all of life, including our spirituality.

For now, it is my sincere wish that what is written here may benefit you on your journey to realizing all the potential you have for sharing love with another.

Chapter 1

===

The Quest for Love

What love is, in all its mysteriousness, the great poets and novelists have already expressed far more eloquently than I could. This book is not about love itself, but about how to find it.

Love is the energy that connects us to other people and to life itself. Even though we all inhabit separate bodies, there are times when this sense of separation dissolves. This can happen within a group – at work or in sport, at family gatherings or amongst friends – and it can happen between individuals or in nature. The experience of love can, at times, be something quiet and unspoken, and at other times blissful and euphoric.

Love is nourishment for the heart and soul. Without it we feel our separation from others as painful and lonely. We may live a life of physical comfort, with lots of activity to stimulate the body and mind, yet we will still feel acutely that something is missing.

We need to understand what that ache of 'something missing' is. We may attempt to dull it through work, food, sex, alcohol, entertainment etc., yet in our most honest moments we know that we are just trying to distract ourselves, and that none of these things will satisfy our deepest need.

The quest for love starts when we admit this need to ourselves, and make a decision to do whatever is necessary to find the love we long for. So long as we continue to distract ourselves, and deny our needs, nothing can happen. Once a clear decision on our part is made, then life starts to support us in all sorts of surprising ways – as if it had just been waiting for us to ask.

The heart and soul will never be satisfied with the mundane.

The dissatisfaction we feel with the ordinary, material things of life is not a trivial thing. It is what in India was known as 'divine discontent' – the discontent that the soul feels with life in its purely physical, earthly form. It is the voice of the divine within us, motivating us to go and find that which we are longing for.

Divine Discontent

When we feel discontent with our lives, we often misinterpret this feeling. We think our dis-satisfaction comes from the fact that our outer circumstances are not as good as they could be. If we could just get a better job, a bigger house and so on – then satisfaction will be ours. Yet if we do manage to improve our circumstances, we often find that, after an initial euphoria, our discontent returns. We may even acquire all the trimmings – the harbour-side apartment, wardrobes filled with Armani and Versace labels, the platinum Amex, gold Rolex and so on. The surface of our lives may become beautifully decorated, and our self-image highly polished, yet the effort to achieve all this will only exhaust us, and alienate us even further from ourselves.

Many people have become so mesmerised by outward appearances that they no longer feel what is happening inside. Whatever sense of discontent they may have is ignored, or not given any credibility. They may think it is due to some quirk in themselves that they can't be as happy as everyone else seems to be. We seem to have lost all ability for self-reflection and self-analysis.

Our society has become characterised by the search for satisfaction in material things. In ancient India, when people spoke of 'divine discontent', there was a clear recognition that the material things of life could not satisfy the needs of the heart and soul. Nowadays, this clarity of understanding is much less common. Instead, we live in denial of our feelings, and we barely know what is happening in our hearts, or what our needs on this level are.

When this connection with the heart is missing, our lives lose direction. Our relationships suffer, our intuition no longer guides us and we lack a sense of purpose and meaning. We become more centred in our heads than in our hearts. As a result, we approach our relationships and all of the dilemmas and perplexities of life in an analytical and cerebral way. We rely more and more on our intellects to solve all of the problems in our lives, including matters of the heart.

The brain and the heart are two very different organs. Our intellect can solve practical problems – even very complex ones – but not issues related to the heart. A different sensitivity and awareness is required for this. Using the intellect to deal with the heart is like using a computer to open a bottle of wine. A computer may tell you that a corkscrew is needed, and even where to buy one, but it won't open the bottle for you. Unless you take the necessary steps to get hold of a corkscrew and use it, your love will remain all bottled up.

The first step that anyone who is interested in the wine of love will need to take is some self-reflection. To reflect on what the values are that are guiding your life at present, and to honestly admit how your current lifestyle makes you feel. To give up any denial, and be unafraid to acknowledge discontent, if it is there.

Some intelligent reflection will reveal to you the same ancient truth – that no matter what the material circumstances of your life are, nothing on the material plane is capable of giving you what you need on the heart level. The starting point in the quest for love is the acknowledgement of our 'divine discontent' – our coming to recognise that material things never give any lasting satisfaction. Then the search for the corkscrew can begin.

Love and Soul's Purpose

If love is missing from our lives, it is not necessarily a sign that something has gone 'wrong'. Often, it is a part of our soul's purpose to experience the absence of love. It is said that you don't know what you've got until it's gone – and this is certainly true about love. It is my belief, and the essence of most spiritual teachings, that our spiritual purpose as human beings is to evolve into consciousness. The Buddha, Christ, Lao Tzu, and many others taught that the awakening into consciousness, the flowering into our transcendental Self, is the highest peak of human evolution. The soul incarnates into a

physical body to learn and experience what it needs to on this journey to awakening. One of the most potent methods life has of rais-
ing our consciousness is to deprive us of something that we have
been taking for granted.

So at times we find ourselves without personal power, or freedom, or love, or any other aspect of ourselves that we have so far
failed to fully appreciate consciously. Often, we will co-operate with
this process, neglecting or turning our backs on love in an almost
deliberate fashion. In our ignore-ance of love, we become arrogant,
judgemental and ego-centred. As our vanity grows, so does our iso-
lation. Eventually we find ourselves in a painful place, lonely and
depressed. It may take us some time to face up to this pain, but from
the point of view of our soul's purpose this is exactly where we are
meant to be – lonely, isolated, depressed and hurting like mad.

Eventually, we are forced to face some tough questions. 'How did
I get here?' 'Why am I hurting?' and 'What is missing from my life?'

Once we have recognised what is missing, and admitted our
need for love, our arrogance starts to subside. It is a humbling recognition. This newfound humility opens us up to a recognition of
what life has to offer. The quest to find love becomes a conscious
one, which is what the evolutionary forces of life want us to do – to
become conscious of love. We begin to rediscover love in a conscious way. We learn about the nature of love, how to cultivate it in
different situations, how to express it, how to give and receive it.
And we learn to recognise its value on the heart and soul level – and
to appreciate and cherish it, as and when it arises.

Love and Consciousness

I believe it is fair to say that much of the love we experience in our
lives, both individually and collectively, is unconscious. We don't
really know and appreciate the love we have for someone till they are
gone – either to the other world, or to some other part of this world.

As a society, our understanding about love is still limited – and
this is especially true when it comes to relationships between men
and women. You don't have to look very far to see that the male-

female relationship is not functioning at its fullest potential in our society. A lot of ignore-ance about the nature of love still exists.

This ignorance has its roots in our society's traditional belief in the sanctity of marriage. For both religious and social reasons, our culture was always far more interested in keeping a marriage together, than it was in the wellbeing of the two souls caught in the marriage. Longevity, perseverance, commitment, endurance and diamond anniversaries scored far more brownie points than did the amount of love the couple experienced together. Marriage was like a marathon race – you had to run through the pain to get the prize. The actual process of cultivating love – how this was done – was given little attention. Traditionally, you were left to your own devices to muddle through as best you could.

Those of us who were brought up in such a marital feat of endurance could see from our ringside seats that there wasn't much love going on. These two contenders for the Diamond Anniversary Championship were hitting the wall at regular intervals. At other times they were just hitting each other. Or else chasing each other with malicious intent. It was the Triathlon to end all Triathlons. Fifty years of commitment to a wasteland devoid of love.

Even if this is a slight exaggeration, the point is that there was a considerable amount of ignorance of love back in those bad old days.

Unfortunately, this ignorance still persists to a large extent today. Many people nowadays still consider longevity to be the hallmark of a loving relationship. Love is still equated with commitment. Psychologists and therapists continue to perpetuate this myth. *Men Who Can't Love* by Stephen Carter, and *Why Men Won't Commit* by George Weinberg are two recent books that are based on the assumption that love equals commitment.

While there is a truth in this – love does bring with it a sense of commitment – the commitment that comes from the heart is very different from the kind of commitment that these authors speak about. The difference is subtle, but of profound importance to our understanding of the ways of the heart and the dynamics of a relationship. In this opening chapter I want to look a little more closely at the difference between the two types of commitment. A lack of understanding of this difference is one of the main causes of the confusion many people still have about relationships.

Love and Commitment

One of the qualities of love is benevolence. A genuine love brings with it a spontaneous wish to do whatever we can for the wellbeing of the person we love. In our hearts we feel that we will always be there for them if they ever need us. This is akin to a commitment. But it is a commitment that is freely given. Love of this kind only flourishes in a climate of non-possessiveness, in which the freedom of each person is fully respected. We cannot ask for, expect, or demand a commitment of this nature.

If someone who loves us offers this kind of support, we will be reluctant to accept it from them. Our love for them will be hesitant to burden them in any way. True love, on both sides, is primarily concerned with the happiness of the beloved. Our own welfare is secondary to this. A lover does not consider his or her own personal agenda. Their concern is for the other person.

This doesn't mean that we become martyrs, or that we force ourselves into making great personal sacrifices. It simply means that we have a lot to give, and the other person has inspired in us the wish to give. Lovers are being true to the deepest part of themselves – to what is in their hearts.

For convenience, let's put a label on this kind of commitment. Let's call it the TOC (True to Oneself Commitment).

There is another kind of commitment. This is the traditional committed relationship in which two persons come together, each with their own needs, wishes and personal agenda. Rather than waiting for a sense of commitment to arise between them spontaneously, from the heart, they enter the relationship with a desire or expectation of where they want the relationship to go. There may be an initial attraction, and a falling in love. This will then trigger off their own personal wishes of what they want from the relationship. Here, each person is more concerned with themselves than they are with the other person. One of the people in this relationship will most likely be far more reluctant to make a commitment than the other. There will be a lot of discussion, debate, argument etc. along the lines of 'how much do you really care about me'. Whatever commitment arises out of this situation will be one that is negotiated to satisfy each person's needs. It will not have the same quality of the heart-felt, freely given commitment described above.

Let's call this second type of commitment the TAC (Traditional Agenda-based Commitment).

The TAC is the type of committed relationship that most people enter into. What are the personal agendas that people bring into a relationship of this kind?

The Agenda-based Commitment

The first thing we notice about personal agendas is that what women have on their list is very different from what men have.

In a traditional relationship, the woman's main concern was for security. She was at a financial disadvantage to the man, and relied on a committed relationship to take care of her survival needs. The man wanted sex, and maybe some sort of status. Men had the financial clout, and the woman had the desirable body. They seemed to be perfectly matched! Women were cautioned to withhold sex till the man had made at least a commitment, if not an offer of marriage. A committed relationship was a way in which both partners could get their basic needs met.

Nowadays, the woman's personal agenda has changed. She still wants security, but mostly she can take care of her own financial needs. She is getting more interested in sex for its own sake, rather than as a bargaining chip. However, for her sex and love go hand in hand. She now looks for commitment as a sign of love.

The mistake she makes is to follow her mother's advice on how to go about getting this commitment. Her mother has told her not to trust men, that they are only after one thing, and that she should insist on a commitment to make sure the man has the right intentions (one of authors quoted above, Stephen Carter, offers women the same advice). She is confused about what love is, and how to create love in a relationship. By following mum's advice, she manages to frighten a lot of men away.

Men, nowadays, still want sex. They continue to enjoy a financial advantage over women. They don't feel the same need for security that women feel. Men want freedom, but they also need love and intimacy. However, they are afraid to express this need. Firstly because, being men, they are afraid to express any sort of need or vulnerability. And secondly, because they fear that if they do express this need, their partner will ask for a commitment from them. Not a TOC commitment, but a TAC commitment, which is something that is very low on their agenda. So they use sex as a way of snatching some sort of emotional nurturing for themselves, and remain very guarded about what is happening in their hearts.

What happens in a conventional TAC type relationship is that whatever love was there at the beginning starts to decline. At first, there was no commitment. There was an attraction, and a mutual discovery of compatibility. A romantic glow developed. The two people fell in love. There was delight in each other's company, perhaps following on from a period of personal aloneness. All of this happened spontaneously, with no expectations.

Then our social conditioning, and our own fantasies about love, step in. If the pink-bubble romantic glow continues to appear in the next few meetings, thoughts about the future start to occupy us, and the question of commitment comes up. 'Will the relationship last?' 'Will he/she want to commit?'

When a commitment is finally agreed to, then the actual love that is experienced in the relationship usually starts to decline. The main reason for this is that the commitment came from the head rather than from the heart. No space and freedom was given to allow a sense of commitment to develop within the heart. Each person has been more concerned with his or her own needs rather than with cultivating love.

Another reason love declines in a conventionally committed

relationship is that we continue to expect it. At first, the pink bubble world arose spontaneously. We were not thinking about it, or expecting it. *It is the nature of love to be spontaneous and to be experienced in the Now.* In a TAC relationship, when we commit to someone, as well as committing to practical sharing and support, we are making a promise that love will continue to arise spontaneously in us in the future. We are confused about what we can realistically expect from this kind of commitment, and what we cannot. Obviously, this is a promise that is impossible to fulfil.

When the future arrives, what do we do? We could be in any sort of unforeseen condition – overstretched at work, depressed, coping with sick parents, facing bankruptcy. At best we can try to fulfil our promise. We share the shopping and the cooking. We try to be caring and attentive. We continue to give practical support. We go to the movies together. But we find that less and less of our hearts are involved in these activities. Our mutual support becomes a kind of a trade off. Rather than giving from the heart, we start keeping score of who has done what.

We feel our partner slipping away emotionally. If they give attention to someone else, we get jealous. Arguments develop. We want to know where they have been, why they are late. The pink bubble world is almost completely gone. In its place there is at best a sense of domestic comfort and security, and at worst frustration, demands and hostility.

This is the reality of most conventionally committed relationships. A committed relationship is not the pot of gold at the end of the rainbow that we imagine it to be. A relationship of this kind only makes sense if what you want is security and the sharing of financial burdens. Usually the man gives financial support and the woman gives emotional support. This is OK as far as it goes. Some people are reasonably content with this kind of arrangement. One should however, be clear about what this kind of relationship can and cannot deliver. It may deliver security, but rarely love.

It is true that we all need a sense of security in our lives – a place to live, an environment that is safe, financial stability and so on. However, as we will see in the next chapter, these needs have nothing to do with the heart. They are basic survival needs. The conventional form of commitment that many people seek in a relationship can take care of these needs for security. The needs of the heart, however, are something very different. A simple act of commitment to a relationship is no guarantee that the needs of the heart will continue to be met. In fact, the opposite is more likely to be the case.

Some people will say that 'If he loved me, he would want to take care of me'. This may be true if the love is equally present from both sides. But if one person senses that the other has an agenda, however unspoken, then their generosity is likely to come under some fairly thorough re-assessment. Furthermore, romantic love is a superficial kind of love. It lacks stability and depth. In the beginning it gives rise to dreams and fantasies, and by the end of the honeymoon it has mostly evaporated. It is not the sort of love that will give rise to the heart-felt sense of commitment we have spoken about.

Holding someone to a promise they have given under these circumstances is harmful to both persons. By not respecting and honouring the other person's freedom, you are also denying and foregoing your own freedom. There is always a quiet resentment that accumulates in someone who is obliged to keep a commitment they no longer feel in their heart. At the same time, you are foregoing your own freedom to find a love that is willingly given and shared. More harm has been done, in terms of accumulated resentment, by people following 'obligations' than by those following their own freedom and soul's purpose.

Non-committed Relationships

There has been a recognition in some sections of the community that conventional TAC type relationships don't give the heart a chance to blossom – that they are too prone to strangling the love that is there with expectations, possessiveness and so on. In recent times, some people have moved away from commitment in relationships. Different ways of relating are being explored in which the couple are together, but in a non-committed way – serial monogamy, open relationships, relationships with separate living arrangements etc. However, as anyone involved in these kinds of relationships will testify, just removing the commitment clause from a relationship is no guarantee that a loving connection will flourish.

What tends to happen in non-committed relationships is that, when issues and disagreements arise, rather than facing them and working through them, we project our sense of discomfort/uneasiness onto the other person. We start to blame them for making us feel less than great. We find some fault in them, and convince ourselves that it is their shortcomings that are making us feel bad. We are unwilling to recognise that, if we feel bad, it is almost always our responsibility. Even if our partner has some shortcomings, as they inevitably will, it is *our lack of tolerance and acceptance* that makes us feel bad – not their shortcomings.

To leave a relationship when things are not going well is to avoid one of the great opportunities that relationships provide – the opportunity to grow. While there are individual differences between people, and we will have more compatibility with some than with others, it is also true that in each woman you will find all women and in each man you will find all men. So once you have found someone compatible, it is best to stick with them and work through your issues – until you can love and accept the other person as much as you love and accept yourself. Otherwise, if we leave them and start looking for someone else, we are just postponing the inevitable moment when our issues have to be faced.

There is more to creating love than simply giving space and freedom. It is a good beginning, but if relationships between men and women are to evolve into a more genuinely loving connection – something that many people are now searching for – then more understanding about the nature of love, and how to cultivate it, is required.

The Quest For Love

What, then, is to be done? We may recognise the desirability of a TOC type of relationship, and the futility of the TAC type. Yet if we are like the majority of people, we also recognise that our actual relationships have been more like TACs than like TOCs.

This is where the quest for love comes in. We begin the quest for love with the recognition that we have not yet attained the kind of opening of the heart that we aspire to. We make the TOC type of relationship one that we aspire to experience. We set about informing ourselves as to how love of this kind can be attained. We recognise that the conventional type of commitment in a relationship is not going to bring us the love we want, and we make a decision NOT to introduce this into any of our future relationships. We may negotiate commitments of a practical nature, but never of an emotional nature. If such a commitment is part of our current relationship, we negotiate a way out of it with our partner. If we have a commitment in our current relationship to providing practical support – house payments, child support etc. – we continue to fulfill this commitment. However, we make it clear to our partner that whatever transpires between us on the level of the heart can only do so in a climate of respect for each other's freedom. And from now on we will not be available to any demands or expectations from them of an emotional nature. Neither will we place any further expectations of this nature on them.

The quest for love is a commitment to find the truth of love, and to express this in one's life. It is a willingness to honestly examine our own ignorance and blind spots, and to give them up and embrace the truth. It is precisely because there still exists today a lot of ignorance about love, and because we manage to block love in all sorts of unconscious ways, that it has become meaningful to speak of a quest for love.

The quest for love is a heroic quest. We are battling against our own unconscious tendencies, against a lot of personal and cultural baggage, against popular public opinion, and even at times against our partner's blind spots. However, when we remain true to love, and our partner starts to recognise this, an unshakeable strength of spirit starts to arise in us, and we gain a new and deeper appreciation in their eyes.

This is the kind of commitment that we can now offer each other – a commitment to create and cultivate love. The traditional form of commitment will not work. Hopping from one partner to another without commitment also does not work. A relationship in which both partners are committed to understanding themselves and exploring the true nature of love, in a mutually respectful and trusting way, will bring about a transformation in both – a transformation from unconscious into conscious lovers. We can call this kind of commitment the TIC (Transforming the Inner-self Commitment).

From a TIC to a TOC

The TIC commitment is a transitional one – a commitment to transform ourselves from the TAC state to the TOC state. We are using a TIC to get to the TOC. This is the essence of the quest for love – to give up TAC and go TIC-TOC. And you will find that after only one TIC-TOC, the clock stops. We enter the timeless dimension of love.

Love is an opening of the heart to someone or some thing. It is a dissolving of the sense of separation between ourselves and another. This connecting with another is something that is both timeless, and that comes and goes in time. When it happens, time stops. We find ourselves deliciously suspended in a timeless Now. Only this moment exists. The wonder of love is its immediacy, its ability to make us feel fully alive in the present.

In the Now, we catch a glimpse of the eternal – the dimension beyond time. We have the sense that this moment could go on forever. When we open our hearts to someone, and share love, a kind of magical foreverness envelops us, in which time ceases.

The Male and Female TIC

The quest for love will in many respects be the same for both men and women, but there will also be some differences.

For men it will be easier to give up the TAC type of relationship. It will be a relief for them. The difficulty for men will be taking on the inner exploration involved in a TIC relationship.

For women, the opposite is true. They will find greater difficulty in giving up the security of a TAC relationship. However, the work of inner exploration, and transforming one's attitudes and feelings about the nature of love is something that will come more easily to them.

Hence men and women can be of great assistance to each other in a TIC relationship. The man can help the woman give up her attachment to the TAC aspects of a relationship. He does this by simply being firm in refusing to accept from her any of her habitual tendencies to form attachments, to be possessive, and especially to ask for a commitment to the future. He can help her to remain in the Now, in the present moment, and refuse to indulge her tendency to seek emotional security for the future.

At the same time, the woman can help the man to get more in touch with his feelings in the Now. To acknowledge and accept with honesty what is going on inside him. To stop him from glossing over, rationalising or denying his feelings. The first step in trans-forming oneself is to honestly recognise and accept where you are right now. Feelings only happen in the Now. Getting in touch with feelings brings us into the Now. Honestly expressing feelings opens us up – it makes us vulnerable. This is where men have the most difficulty – yet love can only be shared in a state of vulnerability.

So the role of both partners is to keep each other in the Now. By staying in the Now, we are creating the right conditions in which the heart may open. Love only happens in the Now. It will be easier for a man to open up in the Now if he knows that it is not going to tie him down to a lifetime of demands and expectations. And it will be easier for a woman to open up in the Now, if she feels that her man is right there, present with her, offering her what is in his heart.

The challenge for men will be to bring transformation to their sexual energy. To raise their energy from the sex centre to the heart. It is not enough for a man just to honestly share with his partner that he is feeling turned on. To be a slave to sex is to be a slave to one's biology, to one's basic instinctual nature. If one is a slave to one's biology, one is at the same level that animals are. This condition lacks any sort of human dignity or nobility.

Men need to reclaim their manhood. This means to reclaim their right to be free to love. To resist the woman's enslaving demands for a commitment, and to insist on his right to find love in his own way – not for her sake, but for his own.

To offer a traditional commitment to a woman is not heroic – it is weak. You are just trading your freedom for regular sex. Even if your woman has insisted on it, she will not respect you for it. Intuitively she will sense your weakness, and you'll be one more rooster whose only reward for all his troubles is to be hen-pecked.

However, once she recognises your strength, and your commitment to transforming your energy and to be true to love, her attitude to you will change.

The challenge for women is to transform their fear-based need for security into love. Fear is a woman's biggest enemy, and greatest challenge. It comes from the same over-identification with the physical body that the man has. Men get attached to the sexual instinct in the body, whereas women get identified with its survival instinct – but both are stuck with the instinctual, animal side of their nature.

In the PR war between the sexes, women have managed a huge victory. They have managed to make their fear-based desire for commitment look respectable, while at the same time making the man's sex based desires look mean and selfish. Women need to understand that their fear-based desire for commitment is as self-centred as a man's sexual desire – and to see that it is not going to bring them any love. They need to develop the strength and the trust to give it up, and transform their fear into love.

So the quest for love for both men and women is simple. Simple to say, but not easy to do. For the man, it is to transform his sexual energy into love. For a woman, it is to transform her fear into love. Of course, this is speaking in generalities, and there will be exceptions to this. Every man has his share of fear, and every woman has her share of sexuality. For each, it is both fear and sexual attachment that needs to be transformed.

How this can be done is what the rest of this book is about.

How To Use This Book

The remaining chapters of this book are structured according to the Tantric yoga chakra system. The seven chakra system itself is very simple, and is explained in the next chapter.

The system divides each person into seven levels, with each level having its own energy, drives and so on. Not only does it give us a clear way of understanding ourselves, but it shows us how our basic energies and drives – such as sex and survival – can be transformed into higher ones, such as love and spirituality.

The quest for love becomes fulfilled at the fourth level, which is the level of the heart. As more energy reaches to and awakens the heart, our relationships take on a completely different quality, one in which our hearts feel nourished and content.

Beyond the fourth level, at the last three chakras, our energies turn to creativity and spirituality. These levels are beyond the scope of this present book, and will be the subject of a second volume in this series.

In some respects each of us is a unique individual, and in other respects we are all the same. I have tried to make the discussion of the different levels of our being, and the suggestions for transforming their energies, as universal as possible. You will need to discern how to apply them to your own situation in a way that suits your individual needs and characteristics.

Chapter 2

The Chakras

'In yoga, *prana* is the life-energy of the universe. There are
three principle channels through which this life-energy
flows, located left and right of, and central to, the spinal
column. These three channels meet at seven different
places along the body. Each meeting place forms a centre,
which is round like a wheel. Indian spiritual philosophy
calls these centres *chakras*. The seven centres are
muladhara, svadisthana, manipura, anahata, vishuddha, ajna
and *sahasrara*. They are not part of the gross physical
body, but exist as part of our subtle energy body.'
– Sri Chinmoy, Yoga Master

The ancient yogis of India, in attempting to understand the complexities of human nature, developed a view of human beings in terms of seven layers – known as chakras.

Each chakra relates to one of the seven basic energies of our human nature – survival, sexuality, power, love, creativity, wisdom/ insight, and consciousness. They are located along the centre of the body, just in front of the spine. The word 'chakra' is a Sanskrit term meaning wheel. In the Tantric yoga system, it refers to a vortex of energy, located at various points along the body. (See *Figure 1*)

Each chakra has its own vibrational frequency, colour, sound, as well as physical and psychological aspects. (See *Table 1*)

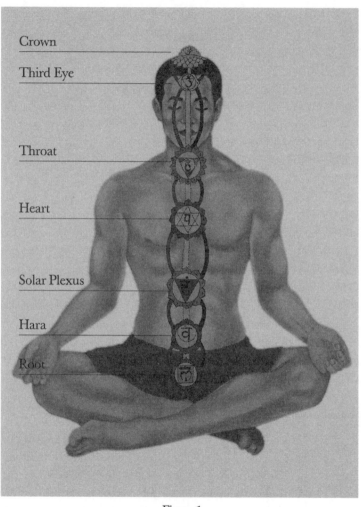

Figure 1

CHAKRA	COLOR	LOCATION	GLAND	QUALITIES
Root	Red	Base of Pelvic Area	Gonads	**Survival** *Security, money, work, finances, fear, anger*
Hara	Orange	Lower abdomen	Testes Ovaries	**Sexuality** *Procreation, passion, jealousy, possessiveness*
Solar Plexus	Yellow	Upper abdomen	Adrenals	**Power** *Assertiveness, control, joy, sadness*
Heart	Green	Centre of chest	Thymus	**Love** *Longing, trust, peace, forgiveness*
Throat	Blue	Throat	Thyroid	**Creativity** *Self expression, speech, honesty, communication*
Third Eye	Indigo	Centre of forehead	Pituitary	**Wisdom/Insight** *Understanding, perception, clarity, cognition*
Crown	White	Top of head	Pineal	**Consciousness** *Connection to Higher Self. Relationship to universe/God*

Table 1

The first thing we notice about the chakras is that we don't find them on the dissecting table. Even though they are located at specific areas of the body, they are not physical entities. Chakras are made up of the stuff called energy. To understand them, we need to understand something of the body's energy system.

Chakras and Bioenergy

To the Western mind, the existence of energy in the body is not something we are familiar with. In Eastern cultures, it is commonly recognised that bioenergy, or the life force, is a vital part of a person's make-up. In the West, our view is more blinkered. The scientific and medical community only recognises the existence of those things that can be measured by an instrument. If it shows up on a Geiger counter, or amp meter, or some other measuring device – it exists. If it doesn't, then its existence is unproven and merely a matter of speculation. So, while we have made great advances in our knowledge of the physical world, we have turned a blind eye to a number of essential, non-physical aspects of life, including the existence of bioenergy.

In China, the existence of the acupuncture meridians has been known for thousands of years. A whole system of medicine was founded, based on a network of energy channels in the body. Energy was found to flow along the meridians. The Chinese called this energy 'chi', and a direct relationship between energy and health was found to exist.

Similar discoveries were made in a number of other cultures – Hawaiian, Tibetan, Japanese, Indian. In our Western culture, there was much promising research carried out several decades ago by a psychiatrist and medical researcher by the name of Wilhelm Reich – a pupil of Sigmund Freud.

Freud had postulated the existence of the libido – which for him was a metaphor for the life force, and in particular the sexual energy. Reich discovered that the libido was more than just a metaphor – it had an existential reality of its own. He called it 'orgone', or bioenergy, and demonstrated in many experiments and therapeutic case studies the direct relationship between bioenergy and sexual and emotional health. This research was carried out in the 1930's and 40's, in Europe and the USA. Because of Reich's interest in the relationship between bioenergy and sexuality, his work was banned by the FDA in America, and he was jailed on fraud charges. Many of his research documents were confiscated and destroyed, and he died after two years in jail, a broken man.

The scientific and medical community has since then put most of its research efforts into pharmaceutical solutions to health problems. The work that was being pioneered by Wilhelm Reich has not been taken any further, except in certain areas outside of the medical establishment. These include the school of Bioenergetics founded by Alexander Lowen, a doctor and psychiatrist, and student of Reich, and similar therapeutic institutions founded by people such as Charles Kelly, Stanley Kelleman, Gerda Boyeson, Ron Kutz and others. In recent years, authors such as Carolyn Myss (*The Creation of Health; Anatomy of the Spirit*) have explored the relationship between the energy of the chakras and health.

My understanding of bioenergy has come from my studies in acupuncture (with Dr J R Worsley at the College of Traditional Acupuncture, UK) and bioenergetic psychotherapy (with Gerda Boyeson at the Centre for Bioenergy, London). I travelled to India on several occasions, and received teachings on the chakras there from three different sources. Sri Dharmakirti, a close disciple of the Dalai Lama, introduced me to the Tibetan Buddhist tradition. Swami Nityananda, at his ashram in Bidadi just outside of Bangalore, taught me the Tantric yoga chakra system, and Osho, a spontaneously enlightened mystic living in Pune, taught an eclectic system based on Taoist, Tantric and other sources. Each of these teachers emphasised the link between bioenergy and the chakras.

Chakras, Energy and Psychology

Wilhelm Reich and the teachers of the Tantric yoga chakra system are agreed on one thing – our energy influences both our thinking and our feelings. If our thinking is in harmony with our true nature, then our energy will be balanced and harmonious. If our energy is balanced and harmonious, our feelings will also be in harmony – relaxed, joyful and filled with a sense of wellbeing.

Feelings and sensations in the body are dependant on the movement of energy. In trying to understand energy, we can compare it to electricity. When electricity moves through a radiator, it produces heat. When it moves through a light bulb, it creates light. Similarly, when bioenergy moves through the second chakra, it produces sexual feelings. When it moves through the heart chakra, it creates love.

This free movement of energy in the body, and the different feelings it produces, can only occur if our thinking is in harmony with the true nature of each chakra. If our thinking is distorted by illusions, misunderstandings and so on, it creates blockages in the flow of energy. We then find that our feelings are affected – we get fearful, or tense, or sexually anxious or mistrustful at the heart.

So throughout this book, as we explore how to use this model of the chakras to understand relationships, we will be focussing on two aspects of each chakra – the psychological aspect, and the energetic/ feeling aspect.

By understanding the *psychology* of each chakra, we are bringing our thinking into alignment with the true nature of that chakra. This helps the energy of that chakra to be natural and harmonious and free. By connecting with the *energy/feeling* of each chakra, we learn two things: firstly, if our feelings are negative or stuck, it tells us that our thinking is not yet aligned with our true nature; and secondly, if our feelings are positive it confirms that our thinking and our actions are in harmony with our true nature. Our energy/feelings are a direct and immediate feedback about the wisdom of our thoughts and the appropriateness of our actions.

So the chakras allow us to gain a better understanding of ourselves in a more systematic way. This understanding is important if we want to have a successful relationship – if we don't have some idea of who we are, how can we share ourselves with someone else?

Our true nature consists of three layers – from the animal instincts of survival and sexuality at the first two chakras, to the human level of personal power, love and creativity at the third, fourth and fifth, through to the divine aspects at the sixth and seventh.

What makes the chakra system such a helpful model is that it is both comprehensive and non-judgemental. It recognises the animal side of our nature without condemning it. It also recognises our humanity and our spiritual potential.

The model has the added benefit of showing us how our basic energies can be transformed. This is where its real value lies.

Chakras and Transformation

One of my teachers claimed that, for the majority of people, 80% of their energy is caught up at the first two chakras. In other words, most of us are pre-occupied with survival and sex most of the time. This is perhaps a rather pessimistic view of humanity, nevertheless I believe it is fair to say that survival and sex take up more of our attention than any of the other chakras.

What this means is that our bioenergy remains stuck at the first two chakras. In the first chapter we saw how most marriages are based on the needs/wishes/desires of survival and sexual issues. We also saw how a transformation of these energies is required if people are to have a greater love and open-heartedness in a relationship.

The model of the chakras shows us how this transformation can occur. Because all of the chakras are linked by their bioenergy, it is possible for energy to move upwards from the lower to the higher ones. As this happens, we become less pre-occupied with survival and sex, and the energies of personal power, love and creativity become awakened. This, in turn, can lead to a further awakening of our wisdom and spirituality at the higher chakras.

TIC TOC Revisited

The commitment to transform the inner self in a relationship involves moving our energies from the lower chakras to the heart. This is probably the most profound, meaningful, and the most fun thing you can do in your life. It involves changing your survival strategies from tedious and fear-based to joyful and trusting.

And it involves making your sexuality more blissful.

Moving energy upwards is not difficult, once you know what you are doing. It requires an understanding of the psychology of each chakra involved, and an ability to tune in to their energies – in the form of feelings and sensations in the body.

We start from where we are. If most of our energy is caught up at the first two chakras, then this is where we start. We make an effort to understand our survival needs, and start to get in touch with our fears and insecurities at this level – as an actual sensation in the lower belly and pelvis. This energetic feeling becomes the raw material for the transformation process. How to transform it into personal power, joy and trust will be described in the next chapter.

Similarly, with sexuality, the first thing we do is try to understand the true nature of the second chakra. Then we start to become aware of the feelings and sensations of sexuality as they arise at the location of this chakra. The bioenergy that is circulating in the second chakra becomes further raw material for transformation. The process of allowing it to rise upwards turns the sexual experience into a blissful one, and provides much of the energy needed to awaken the heart. This process is described in more detail in Chapter 4.

This is the difference between the Tantric yoga approach to creating love, and the traditional Christian approach. Tantric yoga accepts you where you are right now, and starts from there. The traditional Christian approach was to start by trying to be loving – by doing good deeds and being charitable and so on. Sexuality was condemned as sinful, so you had to deny and suppress where you were, and try to be somewhere else instead. This created an inner tension in the form of guilt and sexual repression, and produced a phoney, artificial sort of love. The Catholic Church is still governed by a group of elderly men who are celibate, and does not have a traditional teaching for transforming sexual energy.

The Tantric Yoga System

The teachings of yoga, including the chakra system, are thousands of years old, and were developed by people through a process of meditation and spiritual insight. The path of meditation leads to what is known as 'Sat Chit Anand' – truth, consciousness, bliss. So an essential part of the path of meditation is the search for truth – including the truth of oneself.

Over many years, an understanding of people's true nature – both human and divine – has evolved. This understanding is summarised in the chakra system, and gives us a comprehensive way of understanding ourselves, and the dynamics of our relationships. Knowing how each of the chakras is operating in ourselves gives us a way of knowing ourselves, and sharing ourselves with another person, in a way that is realistic and free of self-deception.

Chakras and You

The chakra system helps you to understand what your needs are on different levels. At the same time, by tuning in to the feelings and sensations in different parts of your body, you will get to know your own individual energy pattern. You will understand where your energy is stuck, where it is in excess, where it is deficient and so on. Your current thinking will reflect this energy pattern, so if the feelings are not immediately present, you can infer their existence by becoming aware of the issues that your mind mostly dwells on.

For example, if your energy is caught up at the first chakra, you will spend a lot of time thinking about money, future security and so on. Your thinking will have an obsessive, worried, anxious quality – it won't leave you alone. If your energy is caught up at the second chakra, your thoughts will have a similar obsessiveness around the subject of sex.

Getting to know yourself means recognising that these thought patterns are a sign of stuck energy – and identifying the feelings and sensations in the body that are driving these thoughts. In the case of the first chakra, this means tuning in to, and feeling, the fear in the lower belly/pelvis that lies at the root of the compulsive thinking about money. Recognising, feeling and admitting to yourself that you are afraid is an important first step in the transformation process.

This is one example of how we learn to recognise the connection between thoughts and energy/feelings in ourselves. As you identify

the feelings associated with each chakra in your body, you will get to
know yourself in a more systematic way. Your inner world becomes
more clearly defined, and it becomes easier to distinguish between
the need for security and the need for love, or between lust and love,
and so on.

Each chakra has its own basic energy. The psychological statement behind these energies is shown in *Figure 2*.

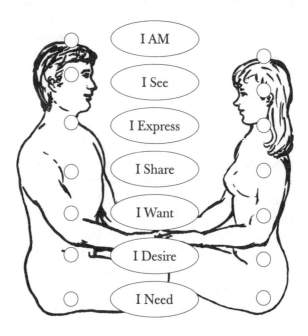

Figure 2

Knowing Yourself

The reality of who we are lies in our energy pattern, and the feelings
it gives rise to. When we are not in touch with our feelings, we can
get carried away with our own imagination about ourselves. For
example, I can imagine that I am not afraid of death. Sitting at home,
having a drink with a few friends, feeling very comfortable, I may
grandly declared to all present that death holds no fear for me. Then

someone challenges me to go and take a bungy jump. I confidently take up the challenge.

As we set off to the jump site, I may still imagine that it is going to be a breeze. Nobody gets killed bungy jumping, so what is there to worry about? We arrive, my ankles get strapped up and we enter the elevator and slowly start our ascent to the top of the tower. As we rise up, my mouth starts going dry, my palms get sweaty, and my heart starts pounding inside my chest. I tell myself this is ridiculous, nobody gets killed bungy jumping – but my body refuses to listen. We emerge from the elevator onto the jump platform, and I look down. My head starts spinning, my brain has gone numb, and my knees and hands are trembling uncontrollably.....

It is not difficult to see which is the more real – my assertion at home, or these feelings on the platform.

There is a saying in bioenergetic therapy that the body doesn't lie. Our feelings, and the energy pattern in the body, will always be a more realistic guide to were we are at, than our thoughts and beliefs. By connecting with the energies of the chakras, we get to know what our real feelings are.

The simplest way to do this is just to place your attention in different parts of your body, and notice, feel and accept whatever feelings and sensations are happening there.

Your feelings will, in turn, reveal to you the ways in which your thinking is not in harmony with your true nature. Before we can adopt a more enlightened way of thinking, we must firstly recognise the thoughts and beliefs we have that are not in harmony – and give them up. Only then does reading and absorbing the material on the chakras presented in this book become helpful. As your thinking becomes more aligned with your true nature, your energies will become freed up, and a sense of being relaxed and at ease with yourself will develop.

We can summarise the process of coming into harmony by the following four steps:
1. Becoming aware of negative feelings and energy patterns (eg. fear)

2. Recognising the corresponding thoughts/beliefs that are not in harmony with our true nature (eg. obsessing about money)
3. Replacing the old thoughts with new, harmonious ones (eg. I now have all I need)
4. Awareness of new, spontaneous, positive feelings

Chakras and Relationships

When two individuals come together in an intimate relationship, a space is created between them that belongs only to them. What happens in that space depends on both of them. They can create a space that is supportive, nurturing, accepting – a haven for the heart and soul. Or they can create a space that is something less than that – a space of comfort and convenience, or a space of mutual ego-stroking, or a battle of wills, or a space of resentment and bitterness.

A relationship is a living thing. It changes its shape and character over time. It passes through different seasons. It has highs and lows. How we deal with these changes, and continue to maintain that living space between us, will determine the course of the relationship.

A relationship's success depends on two factors – mutual compatibility, and a willingness to grow and be open. The first of these happens spontaneously – there is nothing we can do about it, directly, other than making a suitable choice of partner. Indirectly, however, you will notice that the people you attract into your life are generally at a similar level of development to yourself. They mirror your own internal state. If you have a low self-esteem, for example, you will attract someone with low self-esteem into your life – no matter how different they may first appear to be on the surface. Meetings with partners generally follow the 'laws of attraction' i.e. like attracts like. The vibrational resonance of your energy will be attracted to a similar vibrational frequency in someone else. So if you wish to meet someone sincere and open-hearted, it won't just happen by placing these qualities on your wish list. The best way to meet someone like this is to cultivate these qualities within yourself. Otherwise such a meeting is unlikely to occur.

The second factor – the willingness to grow – is entirely in our hands. All living things, including relationships, either grow or stagnate – depending on how they are looked after. So if serendipity, or the universe, has brought us together with someone compatible, then the quality of the space that develops between us depends on what each of us brings into the relationship.

Generally, we will find that relationships bring out the best and the worst in each person. This cannot be avoided – it is one of the reasons why people come together. A relationship is a little bit like a bungy platform – it shows you where you are at, and puts you in touch with feelings you never thought you had. It is easy to experience tranquillity alone in your room, or on the meditation cushion. But these can be lonely places, devoid of love. If we want love in our lives, we have to take up the challenge of a relationship.

There are two main challenges each person must face in a relationship – how to transform the negative emotions of the first two chakras, and how to let go of defensiveness at the heart.

Negative emotions such as fear, possessiveness, jealousy, and the desire to control, are destructive to the space between two people. Unless we know how to transform them, they are likely to undermine all of our relationships.

Defensiveness at the heart blocks the flow of love. Even though the space between us may be undisturbed by negative emotions, if a positive flow of love is not occurring in this space, it is just something empty. It will not nurture or sustain us.

Meeting the Challenges

Growth, or inner transformation, is something that happens as naturally in the inner world as it does in the outer – when we co-operate with it. As we saw in the first chapter, the motivation for growth comes from a sense of dis-satisfaction with our current situation. Rather than using our dis-satisfaction in a negative way – to complain about our life, to blame our partner, or to go into denial – we need to use it positively, as a spur to change and grow.

Your dis-satisfaction is a signal that your thoughts, beliefs and lifestyle are not in harmony with your true nature. Relationships can act as a means of revealing our negative feelings and non-harmonious thoughts.

When this happens, rather than blaming the other person for our bad feelings, we need to take responsibility for them – and thank the other person for making us aware of them. It is almost never the other person who makes us feel bad. Mostly it is our own stuck energy pattern and negative thinking. Blaming your partner is like blaming the bungy platform for making you feel afraid. Your partner is simply creating a situation in which your negative feelings are being brought to the surface.

When you find yourself in this situation, take it as a precious opportunity for self- reflection. You are the only person who can change your inner world, and these are the moments that are most suited to growth and transformation.

To co-operate with your own growth process, there are five things to be understood:

1. You are solely responsible for how you feel in every situation – your partner is never to blame
2. If you feel bad, there are non-harmonious thoughts and beliefs creating the bad feeling
3. You can use your bad feelings to reflect on, and discover, your negative thoughts and beliefs
4. You can replace your negative thoughts and beliefs with positive, harmonious ones
5. Positive, harmonious thoughts will always make you feel good

This is the situation as far as the first main challenge – transforming the negative emotions of the first two chakras – is concerned. How to bring our thinking into harmony with our true nature at this level is what we will explore in the next three chapters.

When it comes to the second main challenge – letting go of defensiveness at the heart – an understanding of the true nature of the heart chakra is required. In chapter 6, we will explore the obstacles that cause defensiveness at the heart, and the ingredients for creating a space in which love can blossom.

Chakras and Spirituality

As our energy reaches to and awakens the heart, new possibilities open up. It is said that God is love, and the heart is the doorway to the divine.

There are three chakras beyond the heart – the throat, the third eye, and the crown. Generally speaking, it is not until the heart has awakened, and we are familiar with how to give and receive love, that these higher chakras become activated.

One of the things that happens is that the energies of the heart start to expand outwards, beyond the limits of a one-to-one relationship. Our love reaches to others around us, and to nature and life itself. This expanding love gives us a new connection with, and awareness of, all of life. We get to know people and nature in new ways. Insights arise into the true nature of the human condition and the natural world. This new wisdom and insight is a sign that energy is reaching to and awakening the third eye.

As it does, it passes through the throat chakra. Here we discover our own individuality, and find our own unique expression for the energies of the heart.

At the third eye, we also come to a clearer understanding of ourselves – our true nature, the role of the ego, and who we are beyond the ego. Our relationship to the universe, and to the divine, becomes more clearly comprehended. Finally, a dissolving of the small self, and a merging with the Clear Light Mind of Buddhahood, becomes possible at the crown chakra.

It is beyond the scope of this book to go into the energies of the last three chakras in detail. They will be the subject of a second book in this series.

In a Nutshell

REALITY CHECK FOR LOVERS

1. We are here to learn to love and discover our true nature
2. We need others on this journey of discovery
3. Being human means "I still have blind spots"
4. Relationships are one place where we discover our blind spots
5. Relationships are an opportunity for growth – for both people
6. Relationships are not about changing the other person – they are about transforming yourself
7. Growth and transformation take us closer to our true nature
8. Our true nature is love, which is the doorway to the divine
9. The path to the divine is as sacred as the divine itself
10. Relationships are sacred spaces

Chapter 3

Survival

The energies of this first chakra enable us to take care of our survival needs. They concern our working lives, money and how we use it, and fears about survival. It is the first rung on the ladder to love, and is relevant insofar as it can either be a stepping stone, or a stumbling block. Some people are able to keep their survival needs in perspective, but many get stuck here. We get so caught up in our working lives, we no longer have the time or the energy to pursue our real interests in life.

The modern corporate and business culture that surrounds us doesn't help. In fact, a strange thing has happened in recent years. Technology was meant to ease our working lives. Machines used to be called 'labour-saving devices'. There was a lot of talk in the 1960's about how technology would soon bring us so much leisure time. Well, take a look at the weary faces on any commuter train at around 7.00 or 8.00 pm, and you can see that this leisure time has so far failed to arrive.

What happened? Why aren't we all out having picnics? Let's step back a little and take a look at this corporate culture we are all so immersed in.

Modern Working Life

The corporate world has imposed its agenda and its values on people's working lives in many ways. The way we work is now controlled by the CEO's and their project managers. In many businesses and industries, the daily schedule and/or target date for a project is planned by a project manager based on a minimum number of employees working a maximum number of hours. The aim is to finish the project as soon as possible, so it will start to generate income. The bottom line is, as always, to maximise profit. People are secondary to this.

As a result, in spite of earning more than at any previous time in history, people have less freedom and leisure time to enjoy their wealth. A working person now typically gets up early (6.00-6.30am), watches some breakfast TV as they prepare for work, spends 30-60 minutes travelling to work, arrives at their desk by 8.00-8.30am, works till 6.00-7.00pm, picks up a take-away dinner, and arrives home between 7.00-8.00pm. The dinner gets microwaved, and they watch an hour or two of television before going to bed. This daily cycle is repeated 5-6 times per week, and their one day off is used to clear out the empty take-away containers, and squeeze in a bit of social life. If the project is falling behind schedule, it is not the schedule that gets adjusted – you are expected to stay back longer.

In spite of all the advances in technology, and the glut of 'labour-saving devices' we now have, people are busier than ever before. As a result, stress, depression and fatigue levels are growing every year. Leisure time consists of taking a 5-minute nap in the office at lunchtime. People now live to work, rather than work to live.

Nobody wants to live like this, but people are so in the grip of unconscious survival fears that they willingly surrender to this dehumanising corporate culture. Add to this their desire to possess all the gizmos of our consumer society – luxury apartment, designer clothes, mobile phones with DVD downloads – and one has the perfect combination (fear and desire) to ensnare the unwary.

The demands of the corporate world are often unspoken. One is simply expected to stay back late, to produce more, to achieve more. The culture is very competitive, and if one wants to get recognition, and to get ahead, one must follow the unspoken rules. Otherwise, you may find yourself dropped from the next project.

This is the most insidious form of slavery. In spite of all of our so-called freedom, human rights, labour reforms etc., we are more enslaved to the greed of the corporate world than ever before. In government departments, hospitals, schools and other public services, the same thing is happening – economic rationalism, privatisation and outsourcing are all creating a climate where people work longer and longer hours, and have less and less leisure time to actually enjoy the wealth they acquire.

All this has great implications for many aspects of our lives. It becomes increasingly difficult to take care of our basic needs. Our diets are poor. We don't exercise (only 26% of adults in the US exercise the minimum recommended amount), we lack a sense of wellbeing – in fact we are constantly tired, stressed and out of sorts. Depression is now at higher levels than it has ever been (19 million American adults – almost 10% of the population – suffer from depression each year). We overeat to cheer ourselves up, or drink to relieve the stress (stress-related disorders cause more lost productivity in the workplace than does depression). Our personal lives and relationships are neglected.

Nothing exists in a vacuum. We are all influenced by the environment we live in. How can two people devote time to creating a loving relationship if they are constantly busy, fatigued, stressed and unhappy? The energies that make a relationship function well – sex, love, passion, joy – arise in the body and in the heart. Overwork takes us out of our bodies, and makes us excessively mental and 'all up in our heads'. We lose touch with our feelings. Then relationships just become a battleground between two people, both wanting something from the other, without having anything to give.

Anyone wanting to find love in their lives will need to start making it a priority. You have to break free of this insidious work ethic that has so many people in its grip, and start creating a life for yourself in which love has a chance to blossom.

We don't need a cultural revolution to make this happen. There are many ways in which you can do this for yourself. For example, find a job in which you are hired at an hourly rate. Choose your own working hours. Reduce your spending to those things that you need. After working a few months, take a month or two off. Give up the competition for promotion. Listen to your body, and follow your needs. Take charge of your life. Be content with less. Make wellbeing more important than wealth.

At the other extreme to our culture, practitioners of Tibetan Buddhism will often forsake all material wealth, and spend several years living in a remote hut in the Himalayas. A sponsor will bring them enough food to survive, and they will devote themselves to meditation and devotional practices. If you read some of the literature on what they are doing, you discover that these people spend most of their time cultivating bliss. The literature of Highest Yoga Tantra describes eight levels of bliss, and how to attain them. They have become connoisseurs of bliss. Bliss is then used to cultivate wisdom and compassion.

Viewed from the outside, these people appear utterly poor. They don't have BMW's, or Armani suits, or even a fridge. However, if you could take a peek into their inner world, you would find riches beyond anything we can imagine. Our experience of bliss is limited to the odd occasion when we fall in love, or land a new job. Occasionally, we get a pat on the back from the boss, or we get the project finished on time – and for an hour or two we feel a sense of satisfaction. It's not bliss, it's more like a temporary relief from our normal state of stress and anxiety. But for most of us, this is as good as it gets. Our inner world is so impoverished, we have no idea of what it is to be wealthy on the inside.

Our outer wealth only relieves our exaggerated fear of survival, and feeds the desires of our self image. That's all. The efforts we have to make to attain this wealth are so exhausting, stressful and time-consuming, we are just pouring all of our life energy down the drain, and missing many of the joys and pleasures that life has to offer.

In Koh Samui, Thailand, – where I have been living for the past 2 years – when a house is being built, the work is done without any idea of a schedule or completion date. The men just show up each day, and work in a relaxed, easy-going fashion. They banter and joke, and enjoy themselves as they work. There is no goal, or target-date to achieve. They do whatever they can on each particular day, and leave it at that. There is no sign that they are stressed out by the demands of some project manager. One rarely sees people working like this in our Western culture. Most work here is carried out with some sense of urgency.

In Thailand, it doesn't matter if the house takes two months or three months to complete. In the West – it matters! Someone is going to be on your case if you don't meet the target date. This creates a lot of stress, and kills off all possibility of enjoying the work for its own sake. You can no longer listen to your body, and follow your own natural rhythm – as the men in Thailand do instinctively.

Western corporate culture has become alienated from basic human needs. The culture exists to extract the maximum productivity from people, rather than enhance our health and wellbeing. If we have to suffer in order to earn our living, well that's just how life is. Sanity means being in harmony with the natural world, and with our own nature. Our work ethic is such that we push ourselves beyond what our bodies, minds, hearts and souls are willing to, or capable of, enduring. We have become so blind to our own insanity, we no longer see the condition we are in (22% of the adult population of America – approximately 44 million people – suffer from a diagnosable mental disorder in any given year, including depression, schizophrenia, anxiety, eating disorders and Alzheimer's). How did we get to be this way? Where do all these stress-producing schedules and target dates come from?

They come from the minds of the executives who run the corporate world. These work practices are basically inhuman. They have nothing to do with the needs and natural rhythms of your body, or the natural rhythm of the universe. Rather than being in harmony with people's needs, the corporate world is only ever in harmony with the minds of a few greedy, aging workaholics, whose only satisfaction in life comes from trying to out-perform each other, and boast about it at the next shareholders meeting.

Your Choice

The question for you right now, dear reader, is – do you want to be a pawn in their game, or do you want to actually enjoy your life? Never mind about bliss, let's just start with the modest aim of finding pleasure and enjoyment. Then we will really have something to share with our beloved, when he or she shows up.

This first chakra is about taking care of our survival needs. It is only the first rung on the ladder to love, joy and happiness. Our needs at this level are very simple – a roof over our heads, some food, clothing, a little extra spending money – and that's it! Most of us could take care of those needs in just a few hours a day. We would then have the time and energy available to move up the other rungs of the ladder. The satisfaction we get from taking care of our survival needs is a very paltry thing. It is no more than a relief of anxiety. If we get stuck at this first rung, we are effectively giving up all possibility of any real joy, love or bliss in our lives.

There is a story of a wealthy businessman in India who went to visit a famous yogi. The yogi was living a simple life in a hut, with a few followers in attendance. The businessman approached the yogi and, as is customary in India, touched his feet as a mark of respect. He started praising the yogi for having renounced all desire for wealth and material possessions, what a great spiritual person he must be, and so on, when the yogi interrupted him and said "Wait! You don't understand. It is I who should be praising you. You are the real man of renunciation. My life here is filled with joy and bliss, but when I look into your eyes I see only poverty and nothing else. So tell me, my friend, which one of us has really renounced?"

It is becoming increasingly rare to meet people with this kind of understanding nowadays, even in India. I recently spent a few months in Delhi at the invitation of a businessman friend of mine. We had met at an ashram in Nepal, where we were both staying. When he heard that I practiced healing and spiritual counselling, he invited me back to Delhi as his guest, to do some work with him, and some of his friends. He introduced me to his social circle, a section of the well-to-do business class of Delhi society, several of whom I started to work with.

They would send their chauffer-driven cars to my apartment to pick me up, welcome me into their homes with cocktails and lunches of the finest Indian dishes, and usher me into their private drawing rooms for our consultations. As I was from outside of their social group, they felt safe to open up their secrets to me, and from at least a dozen or so people in this group, I heard the stories of their private lives. Invariably, their first comments always were "Please make sure nobody ever gets to hear about this", and then there would follow stories of depression, neglect, loneliness, eating disorders, family feuds and unhappy marriages.

I asked several of them "You have been suffering in silence for so long before now. Was there no-one you could turn to for support or guidance?" They all said no – they had lost faith in the traditional yogis, and the medical profession that they now turned to for help could only offer anti-depressant medication.

We are seeing a very rapid spread of Western culture to all parts of the world, and an eroding of traditional cultures and wisdom. The irony of my stay in Delhi was that here was I, a Westerner, teaching a blend of psychology and traditional Eastern wisdom to Indian people, and being feted for it. At one dinner party, I was acknowledged as the 'yogi' of the group, and in a private meeting later, two of the guests asked for my blessing, and touched my feet as they left.

In Thailand now, and in other parts of SE Asia, Western influences are creeping in. An article in the Bangkok Post headlined 'Job Stress Taking a Toll on Thai Men', stated that "…stress from longer working hours because of the economic rebound caused a major increase in erectile dysfunction in Thai men, according to a recent survey."

It won't be long before the project manager is everywhere, planning people's working lives, and the laughter and good humour of the workers on Koh Samui will soon be a thing of the past.

The reason most people get taken in by the demands of the corporate world is fear and greed. We fear job loss more than anything else, and we desire all the trappings of success. Yet in the West, no-one ever starves or dies of malnutrition. Everybody survives. So how rational is this fear?

Survival and Fear

In the past it was not uncommon for someone to work for the same company for 30 or 40 years. People had job security. Nowadays, it is more common to change jobs every few years. Sometimes you choose the change, sometimes the change is forced on you. No one feels secure in their job anymore. Things are always changing. Companies go broke, or get taken over. Mergers happen, new managers come in. Projects finish, the workload goes down, staff get axed. Companies no longer show loyalty to their staff, in terms of keeping them on in lean times. Similarly, individuals think nothing of leaving a company if a better opportunity presents itself.

As a result, people generally feel insecure in their jobs. There are two levels at which this fear of job loss operates – the fear of survival, and the fear of loss of face. Mostly, these fears operate in the subconscious. We barely recognise they are there. We just know that, when threatened with a job loss, we get stressed and insecure, often to such an extent that we feel ourselves becoming overwhelmed.

Fear is in many cases irrational. As children, we are afraid of the dark, of the bogeyman, of ghosts. Faced with a job loss, fear again sends our imagination into overdrive. We see ourselves getting evicted from our homes, we imagine our friends avoiding us, the car gets repossessed, we'll spend weeks sitting on park benches.

It is at this moment that we become the perfect victim for the corporate culture. This fear drives us back into the project manager's arms so fast, he doesn't know what has hit him. At this stage we'll agree to anything – any pay, any hours, any conditions. Anything to avoid the bogeyman and the night sweats!

It is not the corporate culture itself that makes us a victim, we become the victims of our own fear. So long as this fear remains unconscious and unanalysed, it will continue to run our lives. However, as soon as we throw some light on this fear, it starts to dissolve.

Let's look a little more closely at these two fears, and bring some understanding to them. Then we can decide – are these fears really worth getting so worked up about, or can I get over them and give myself the freedom to chose a more fulfilling way to live.

Fear of Survival

Everybody's deepest fear is the fear of death. We all want to avoid death, yet it is going to happen to all of us. Intellectually we know this, but existentially – in the pit of the stomach – we have not accepted it. In our day to day lives we are not even aware of this fear, yet when confronted with the actual threat of death we will react fearfully. If you doubt this, go and take a bungy jump – and see what happens.

If you want to be free of the limitations this fear imposes on your life, you need to firstly bring it into conscious awareness. It is only by avoiding fear that we become the victim of it. Facing it consciously creates the possibility of transforming and overcoming it.

Look at how this fear operates in your life, at a subconscious level. See how it causes you to over-react to life's changing circumstances, how it limits you, how it makes you opt for safety and security, rather than daring to follow your dreams and aspirations. Then ask yourself – do I want to continue to live a life that is dominated by fear, or do I want to be free?

Fear of Loss of Face

This fear is perhaps even greater than the fear of death. Not only do we want to survive, we want to thrive. We want to survive in style!

We live in a society that values material success. We admire those who acquire. In the social standings, the more you possess, the more you progress. This is, of course, absurd, and we have become very ironic about our own superficiality. Yet we remain attached to it, and any loss of wealth or possessions we experience as almost intolerable, as though one of our limbs was being amputated.

Our self image is derived, not just from our body, but from our possessions and the social status they bring us. We don't know who we really are, so we develop a sense of self based on what those around us will recognise and admire. So long as this socially acquired identity remains unquestioned, it will continue to dominate our thinking, and drive us to keep polishing and protecting it, as though it was something of great value.

Then a job loss, or a loss of status, will be experienced as a loss of self – something we want to avoid at all costs.

When these two fears combine, they can cripple us to such an extent that we get stuck at this first rung of the ladder. Then our longing for love will simply become an impossible dream, something we fantasise about, but never take any real concrete steps to attain.

If we want to enjoy life, if we want to be free to find love, then these fears need to be overcome. This is not as difficult as it sounds. Fear is not something tangible that we have to struggle with. Fear is similar to darkness. In fact, it only arises in the dark – either physically or metaphorically. To get rid of darkness, we don't try to drag it out of the room. Darkness has no reality of its own. It is just the absence of light. All we have to do is switch on the light, and it is gone. The same happens with fear.

There are three things which, when switched on, will cause our fears to evaporate. These are understanding, courage and trust. Let's look at each of these in turn.

Understanding

Understanding removes the irrational elements of fear. We see a shape on the road that looks like a snake, and we become alarmed. Closer inspection reveals it to be a fallen branch, and this simple clarity of understanding removes the fear.

It is the same with death. We have no clear understanding of death. We imagine it to be a painful entry into some unknown terrible darkness. Death is still taboo in our society. Whenever somebody dies, it is spoken of in hushed tones, as if the dead person has just committed the ultimate blunder.

Take a close look at that shape on the road called Death, and what you see is a soul being released from a body that it no longer needs. The person doesn't die. Only the body 'dies' – in the sense that it gets left behind. In fact the body was only being kept alive because the soul was inhabiting it. It was already just dead matter, but it remained luminous with the life of the soul. It is like the moon – the moon gives no light of its own, it just reflects light from the sun. So the body merely reflects the life of the soul. When the soul leaves, the inherent deadness of the body becomes apparent.

The problem is, we have become identified with the body, rather than with the soul – and this is our basic misunderstanding, and the cause of our fear of death.

The body is no more than a space suit we have put on in order to explore life on planet Earth. We get very caught up with our space suit. We give it a name, and address. We compare the size and shape of our space suit with other people's, and with ones that we see in magazines. We get obsessed about bits of our space suit – are they too round, too flat, too baggy, too tight......and before we know it we are caught up in the mass hallucination that "this is who I am!" We forget about the person inside, and think we are the suit. Everybody around us colludes with our delusion. They don't ask us "How is your suit today?", or "Where does your suit live?"; they ask "How are you today?" and "Where do you live?" So with every encounter we have, our illusion is reinforced. We end up completely forgetting that we are not the body. And we forget that, as far as the body is concerned, death is inevitable, whereas from the perspective of the soul, no such thing as death ever occurs.

The second misunderstanding many of us have is the idea that we need security and permanency in life. We always want things to last – our jobs, our relationships, our circumstances. We fear change, yet change and impermanence are inevitable. Everything in life is in a state of flux, especially nowadays when the rate of change is actually accelerating. All is impermanent and uncertain. Life circumstances change. Marriages often don't last. People fall in and out of love. Jobs come and go. Change is the only constant in life. If we don't recognise and accept this, out of ignorance we start clinging to people and situations. This clinging is what creates most of our pain and suffering when, unexpectedly, things change. We want to nail everything down around us. Yet if we occasionally do manage this, life becomes dull, predictable, boring and we end up more dead than alive. If we can accept impermanence as a fact of life, we can flow with life's changing circumstances. There may be some sadness as we part ways with something or someone we value, but we get over it, and move on. A life that is lived without clinging has more colour, vitality and richness than one lived in fear of change.

As this understanding deepens, our fears will greatly diminish.

We loosen up. Our life ceases to be a grim struggle to survive. We see it as a play, and the earth as a playground. We can start to listen to the dreams and longings in our hearts, and find the courage to make them happen.

Courage

Understanding is one thing, but it is not enough if we want to be free. There are plenty of armchair gurus out there who never dare to act. To act on our understanding takes courage – it needs guts. Especially if what we aspire to goes against popular opinion.

Even with a right understanding, some fear will still be there – the fear of stepping beyond the safety and security of our mundane lives. The fear of going against the opinion of others, of standing alone and being true to ourselves.

To really start to follow your dreams and aspirations takes guts, you must be willing to take some risks, to act in spite of the fear. It needs a warrior's courage and strength. Without this you will always chose the safe and secure path in life, and never know what love and freedom are.

We develop courage by just being bold and taking some risks. One starts with small steps, and as your confidence grows, so will your warrior's spirit. Eventually you discover the truth of the old saying that 'fortune favours the brave'. The more you follow your heart, the more life will support you, often in unexpected ways. We don't have to play it safe all the time. Life and the universe are not hostile forces that we have to secure ourselves against – they are always friendly and supportive of our real needs and aspirations.

The more we experience this, the more we feel a trust in life starting to arise.

Trust

Understanding is of the head, courage is of the gut, and trust is of the heart. Trust creates our deepest sense of connection with, and confidence in, the benevolence of life. It is only through developing trust in our hearts that we truly feel secure. External forms of security such as jobs, bank accounts, houses, relationships etc. won't do it. We know that any of these things can be lost at any time. Out of fear we cling to them, in an effort to relieve our sense of insecurity – but the very clinging itself only increases our sense of insecurity. No matter how wealthy we get, we'll still be anxiously watching the share market prices every day. The fear still remains. The only antidote to this fear is trust.

What is trust? Trust is not just a mental attitude, it is a state of the heart. Worry, doubt and anxiety all arise in the mind as a result of fear and of old conditioned habits. We worry excessively about things that are beyond our control. We carry in our minds our own agenda, our own wishes and desires about how things should be. But the forces that shape our lives – the global economy, the rhythms of nature, political and cultural changes, karma, other people's agendas etc. are far greater than anything we can control. This is simply the way things are. We can react to this fact of life in one of two ways – we can get anxious and stressed about it, or we can trust that everything will work out for the best.

The intelligent choice is obviously to trust. There is nothing we can do about these things, but trusting helps us to sleep at night, and to enjoy whatever life offers. Doubt gives us sleepless nights, and a lot of unnecessary disappointments.

There is an old Sufi saying "Trust in Allah, but tether your camel first", which sums up very neatly the right attitude to trust. In other words, we have to do our bit, we must make sure we have done all that we can do to make a certain thing happen. God can only work through our hands. Then we let go and leave the outcome in the hands of God or the universe. Which means that, whatever the outcome, we trust that it is for the best – that God doesn't make mistakes.

This way of relating to life is still quite rare in our society. Our forefathers wanted to control and master the forces of nature, rather than co-operate with them. The attitude has always been to dominate and subdue, rather than to trust and co-operate with life. Our conditioning makes it difficult for us to trust.

If you are still unsure which option to choose – try this. Take a good look at yourself in the mirror, and get a sense of your own size and weight. Maybe you're a big guy. Let's say 6'4" tall, and 200 lbs of lean muscle. Then step outside and look up at the night sky. See all the stars twinkling in the distance. Get a sense of the size and scale of the universe. See the forces that hold it together, and the subtle energies that move it. That's what you're up against.

What do you want to do? Do you want to take it on, just like Pa and Grandpa did? Keep up the family tradition? OK, go ahead. Take a swipe. Grab it by the collar and shake it. Scream!! Insist on having things your way.

What happens? Are the stars re-aligning themselves? Is there a white flag being raised out there? There isn't…??!!

A person becomes wise when he or she realises the reality of where they stand in relationship to the universe.

What does it mean to trust in life? It means having the secure knowledge in your heart that life is benevolent, and that the subtle forces and energies that move the universe are always caring for you. It is trusting that you will always be given what you need in life. It is falling in harmony with the universe, letting yourself dance with life. Your part of the dance involves listening to your intuition, following the still small voice in your heart. Trusting that what you hear is what the universe wants to support. Not worrying, not doubting, not feeling anxious – but having the same relaxed, quiet trust that a child has in the support of its' parents.

Harmony with the Universe

As our fear diminishes, we are more able to let go and trust and surrender. At the same time a paradoxical thing happens – we feel more in control of our lives. We are no longer victims of the insecurity that drove us to sacrifice our life to work. We start to follow our true purpose, and find our creativity.

This freedom from fear and insecurity is tremendously liberating. We have started becoming true to ourselves. We are no longer ruled by the mob psychology, instead we become individuals. We can put our survival needs into their proper perspective, and 'tether the camel' in a way that is easy and enjoyable. Life ceases to be a problem. It becomes fun. Work and play intermingle. Rather than being driven by anxiety, you find joy in what you are doing. If you are renovating or building a house, you enjoy the creativity of the experience in each moment. You don't stress about the outcome. You trust that whatever is made out of joy and creativity and love will find a willing buyer. Its energy will attract people.

If you are not enjoying your work, you will leave it – trusting that there is a place for you in the universe where you can express your true purpose in that moment, and be rewarded for it.

Things will happen easily and spontaneously. When you follow your intuition, a whole new world opens up – a world of synchronicity, serendipity, fortuitous meetings and surprising co-incidences.

A few years ago, I came to a dead end in my work as a healer and counsellor. After ten years, my enthusiasm and joy in the work had left me. I decided to take some time out and travel, trusting that whatever I was meant to be doing next would show up. After some months, I accepted an invitation from a friend of mine to visit him in Koh Samui, Thailand. I fell in love with the island as soon as I arrived. Within a few weeks, I met an acquaintance of his, who had just opened a holistic health resort on a quiet beach. He offered me a position there as holistic health consultant and meditation teacher. The perfect house turned up in a coconut grove near the resort. I could not have designed a better lifestyle for myself than the one I enjoy now – living on a resort island, doing the work that I love with a diverse range of people from all parts of the world.

This is not 'luck'. This is allowing the universe to guide you to where you are meant to be.

At the end of this chapter, there are a number of practical suggestions for bringing your life into harmony with the universe.

Surviving Your Survival Needs

It is up to each individual to decide how best to take care of his or her survival needs. Some people find their passion and their purpose in work that brings them a lot of money. Some love writing poetry

– and need a day job to support themselves. How much the 21st century market place values your skills and creativity will vary with each person. Two hundred years ago, poets were superstars, and could earn fortunes. Now you may have to write some advertising jingles to help you pay the bills.

Whatever you decide, it will help to keep the following universal principles in mind:

- The universe is abundant
- There is a place here for everyone
- We each have a unique purpose to fulfil
- Our purpose may change from time to time
- Fulfilling your purpose will bring you joy
- If joy is lacking, you are not aligned with your purpose
- The universe will always support you in fulfilling your purpose
- When you are on purpose, things will flow easily and effortlessly
- Keep your needs simple – the universe will support your need, but not your greed
- You can trust the universe

The more you can let go of your survival fears, and be bold enough to follow your intuition, and trust in the support of the universe, the more your energy will be freed up to enable you to move up the ladder of love and joy.

These principles are not something new. They have been described elsewhere, especially in the writings of Shakti Gawain, Wayne Dyer and Stuart Wilde.

There are many people already living their lives in accordance with these principles, who can testify to the fact that they work. It is possible to live a life of ease, abundance, and joy in the physical world, and still hold true to your spiritual purpose. The more people there are who actually live their lives like this, the greater the field of synchronicity and fortuitous meetings becomes. As more people open up to live in harmony with the universe, the greater is the possibility of their enhancing your life and you enhancing theirs. We enhance each other.

So your breaking free of fear is not something that just benefits you. It benefits everyone. The whole world is enhanced by your decision. It is not just that the universe supports us, but we in turn support the universe. We become co-creators with life and the creative principle.

If you remain closed, fearful and isolated, not only do you suffer – but the whole world suffers. Your input, your contribution will be missed.

People sometimes refer to the so-called New Age movement as the 'me generation' – the implication being that those involved in this way of life are self-centred. Nothing could be further from the truth. The more you follow the old way of doing things, the more isolated and self centred you become. As you start to live in harmony with the universe, open exchanges between yourself and others happen more frequently. Not only do you receive abundance, but you share and contribute abundantly with others. Your contribution no longer consists of destroying the environment in order to produce a lot of useless gadgets. I doubt whether anyone comes here with that as their spiritual purpose. You contribute something that actually benefits others, something of which you can be proud.

WHAT TO DO? – Practical Suggestions for Breaking Free

If you are in a job involving long hours, and find it stressful and fatiguing rather than joyful, start by taking small steps.

- Arrive later and leave earlier
- Change your attitude. Instead of spending money to cheer yourself up, realise what it costs you to earn this money – in terms of time and energy – and start to use that time and energy more creatively and joyfully
- If you are a big spender – make a budget
- Understand your fears and desires, and give them up
- Begin to explore the following suggestions:

1. DISCOVER YOUR INTUITION

The following is a simple exercise to help you to connect with your intuition. Formulate a question in your mind that you want intuitive clarity about. It should be a question that has a simple yes or no answer, for example 'Should I leave this job?".

Sit in a quiet, undisturbed space and begin by checking within yourself – is there any fear or desire associated with either a yes or a no answer. If you notice that, for example, you fear a yes, or desire a no, make a deliberate mental effort to clear these fears/desires from your mind.

With your mind free of fear and desire, extend both hands out in front of you with palms upward. Choose one hand to represent a 'yes', and the other to represent a 'no'. Hold the question in your mind, and allow a spontaneous response to occur in your body, without interference from you. The hand that gets 'lighter' and rises upward represents your intuitive response to the question. Timing is also important. If you get a 'no' answer now, ask another question relating to timing.

2. DREAM AGAIN

Our heart's longings and soul's purpose reveal themselves through the imagination. Get in touch with your dreams and aspirations again. Take some regular time out (1-2 hours, 2-3 times per week). Make sure there are no distractions. Turn off the phone and the TV. Let the time be unstructured. You can either do nothing, or take up a simple task, such as walking, or something creative but undemanding. Ask yourself "What do I want?", and hold this question in the back of your mind. Let yourself daydream, and observe your dreams.

When a daydream or aspiration starts recurring, visualise it happening, and note how it makes you feel. If it regularly makes you feel uplifted, inspired and joyful, then know you are on the right track.

3. LEARN DIVINATORY ARTS

Take a workshop and learn how to read the Tarot cards, or use a pendulum, or read the I Ching.

4. CULTIVATE TRUST

Look at the issue of trust in your life. Is it difficult or easy for you to trust? Are you able to let go and surrender to things that are beyond your control, or are you often trying to manipulate and control people and events to your advantage?

As you discover attitudes and habits that are opposed to trust, begin to let them go. People who are chronically unable to trust may have had a difficult early relationship with their mother. It is through our mother that we experience our first contact with the universe. She represents the universe for us in our earliest years. If this relationship was loving and trusting, it will be easy for us to maintain this trust into adult life. If it was a problematic relationship, it will most likely be difficult for us to trust as adults, and we will need to do some healing work on this relationship before we can regain the ability to trust.

The following are some affirmations that will help to cultivate trust in your life:

- I give up all doubt, worry and anxiety about things beyond my control
- I now trust in the universe
- I trust that my needs will always be met
- I trust that I will always meet the right people and circumstances to fulfill my purpose
- I trust that the universe will always support my purpose and aspirations
- I do all that I can to fulfill my purpose, and trust that the universe will take care of the rest
- I now align my thoughts, actions and words to be in harmony with the universe and with my soul's purpose
- I now align myself with the abundance and prosperity of the universe
- I now allow the grace, joy and abundance of the universe to express itself through me

5. UNDERSTAND THE LAW OF KARMA

As we come to trust and surrender to life and the universe, it is important to understand how the law of karma operates. The law of karma is summed up in the saying 'you reap what you sow'. In other words your actions have consequences. If we have been deceitful or harmed others in the past, there is a natural karmic consequence that we will encounter. We all carry within us uncooked seeds of karma from past actions – either in this life, or from past lives. As our past karma ripens, fortuitous or adverse situations will arise. If we have created good karma, we will meet with good fortune either in the form of wealth, or success, or a loving relationship, or meeting a spiritual teacher, and so on. If we have negative karma to burn up, the opposite will happen – we may suffer a financial loss, or meet with an 'accident', or some other setback. If we understand what is happening, we can meet all of life's circumstances with acceptance and equanimity, without losing our trust in the universe. Burning up bad karma from the past frees us up to find success in the future, and teaches us to respect the law of karma so we don't make the same mistake again.

In order to ensure that our future karma will be positive, we should refrain from any actions that bring harm to others, develop a respect and reverence for all of life on Earth, and practice generosity.

6. ACCEPT DUALITY AND IMPERMANENCE

All of life on earth is dualistic and impermanent. Duality means that everything has a yin and a yang aspect. The person you love (even your soul mate) will sometimes be delightful, and sometimes annoying. The work you love will sometimes be inspiring, and sometimes challenging. In other words, nothing is perfect. We're all going to have good days and bad days. Every person and situation in life has this dual quality. If you can accept this, life gets so much easier. If you can give up hankering for the 'good', and complaining about the 'bad', and accept all of life with equanimity, you save yourself a lot of unnecessary suffering.

Impermanence we have already discussed. It is the failure to recognise and accept these two basic facts of life that creates most of the frustration, bitterness and unhappiness that people experience. By accepting both duality and impermanence, we flow with life, and maintain our trust and joy and good humour.

7. CULTIVATE GRATITUDE

Start to practice being grateful for all that life is giving you. Give up attitudes of complaint, impatience and demand. Recognise the perfection in everything, see the beauty and benediction of the joys and the challenges in life – and be grateful for both.

Chapter 4

═══

Sexuality

In the quest for love, if love is a rose flower, then sex is the sap that rises up from the roots of the rosebush, and brings the flower to bloom. If we don't cultivate the sap – if we don't appreciate and enjoy our bodies and our sexuality – we will find that there isn't much love spontaneously arising in our hearts.

Sex is probably the most fun you can have in a human body. In its natural state, it is pure delight in the aliveness and sensuality of the body, and a joyful surrender to the passion of physical intimacy.

Unfortunately, within our culture, people's experience of sex has often fallen short of this. It is unlikely that our grandparents would have described their experience of sex in this way. Granny was more likely to be thinking 'Oh God, here comes the old rooster again – just when I've put down clean sheets. Oh well, get it over with quickly, will you Pop'. Meanwhile Pop had his eyes closed, thinking 'Ah, Tina Turner – my darling!'

In our society, this second chakra has been the most misused and misunderstood of all the seven chakras. The disturbances and blockages we carry in our sexuality have probably contributed more to the lack of love in our lives than any other factor. To suppress sex is to bonsai the rosebush – we cut its roots and end up with little, stunted flowers. If we can get our sexuality right – that is, in harmony with its true nature – we are half way to creating the love we want in our lives.

In this chapter, we will explore the true nature of our sexuality. There are two aspects to this – the *biological* and the *transformational*. The first of these refers to sex in its natural state. The second aspect looks at how we can transform our sexual energy into higher states of bliss, love and consciousness. Before we go into these two aspects in detail, there are some unpleasant truths about the way our culture has dealt with sexuality in the past that it will be helpful to review.

A Brief History of Sex

The historical origins of sexual suppression are unknown (cf. *The History of Sexuality* by Michel Foucault). However, we do know that Christianity, and especially Catholicism, was at the forefront of the cultural institutions responsible for the suppression of sexuality in the past. It is likely that, when Christianity was seeking to spread its influence, those in power had some instinctual recognition that sexually suppressed people were easier to control. As every farmer knows, a bullock is always more docile than a bull. Hence they declared sexuality to be sinful in all but the most restricted circumstances – within marriage, for the sole purpose of procreation. All other sexual expression was forbidden, under threat of mortal sin, the punishment for which was eternal damnation in hell. People were taught that sex was something shameful, and indulging in it was against the will of God. As the masses suppressed their sexuality, it became easier for those in power to control and manipulate them.

People in the grip of fear, guilt and shame about their most desired and pleasurable bodily function became putty in the hands of the priests. For following their own natural desires, they were condemned by the priests as sinners. The priests then gave themselves the power to absolve people's 'sins' through confession. This made them even more powerful than the State. The State had power over taxes, and even over life and death, but the priests now had the ultimate power – power over the eternal fate of people's souls!

The pretext for all this was morality, yet Christ only ever spoke out against adultery. He never condemned sex as immoral. Similarly, the Ten Commandments have only forbidden adultery (6th), and thinking about adultery (9th). The moral argument is a flimsy one, and in all likelihood hides the real motivation behind Christianity's suppression of sex – the desire for power. Whatever the reasons, the fact remains that sexual expression has been surrounded by shame, guilt and fear within our culture for many centuries.

In recent years there has been a reaction against all this. It started with the counter-culture of the 1960's and 70's and spread through the rest of the community. The invention of the contraceptive pill and hippie slogans such as 'make love not war' led, after some hostility, to an acceptance of pre-marital sex, and the radical notion that sex was something that could be enjoyed without guilt or shame. With the exception of fundamentalist Christians, most people now enjoy a freedom in their sexual expression that was unheard of fifty years ago.

The history of our culture's uneasy relationship to sex still has repercussions for many people. Given the duration and extent to which the suppression of sex has occurred, and the relative recentness of our attempts at liberation, we should not be surprised to find some hangovers from the past that still affect us today.

Many people nowadays are still uncomfortable with their bodies. In addition to being judgemental about its general size and shape, there is a lack of real love and appreciation for the body, and a particular sense of shame and embarrassment about the genital area. We don't often feel a sense of acceptance and delight with our bodies.

A residual sense of fear and discomfort with sex also shows up in the way we give sex education to the young. After a review of 'the facts' of sexual coupling, most sex education focuses on the dangers of sex – of pregnancy, and of catching AIDS and other STD's. There is no mention of how to find pleasure and delight in the expression of sexuality. What we are effectively teaching young people is to be afraid of sex, rather than to enjoy it.

There are other indications of our discomfort with sex. Flirtation has become a thing of the past. A woman's flirting is now interpreted as a 'come on', while a man's flirting is often taken for sexual harassment. One of the negative aspects of our recent attempts at sexual liberation is that a kind of over-emphasis and obsessiveness with sex has arisen. The pendulum is swinging the other way. Pornography, sex-addiction, and a pervasive self-consciousness about sex are all indications that, as a culture, we are still far from natural and at ease with our sexuality.

Without an understanding of the true nature of sex, we are setting ourselves up to repeat the same historical pattern. As the pendulum swings further towards the kind of indulgence, addiction and 'sex as entertainment' that we are now seeing, there will eventually come another reaction against this. People will start once again to condemn sex, and extol the virtues of abstinence and suppression.

A natural sexuality is neither repressive nor indulgent. It does not condemn sex, nor does it crave after it. It simply accepts sexual desire when it arises, and also accepts the absence of sexual desire when it is not there. There is a trust and acceptance of the forces of nature within oneself – that they are rising and falling in exactly the way they are meant to.

With this historical background in mind, we can move on to our exploration of the true nature of sexuality. As I mentioned earlier, there are two aspects to this – the biological and the transformational. For the purpose of getting into harmony with a natural sexuality, it is enough to deal with the first aspect. The second may be considered as an optional extra. The first aspect will bring your sexuality into a natural state, which many people will find more than satisfactory. The second aspect is for those who wish to put some icing on the cake.

In terms of the biological aspect of sexuality, there are seven issues to be considered:
- Sex as Energy
- The Wisdom of the Body
- Control and Letting Go
- Chemistry and Compatibility
- Sex and Romance
- Sex and Love
- The Dark Side of Sex – Jealousy and Possessiveness

In Part 1 of this chapter, we will consider each of these in turn.

Part 1. The True Nature of Sex

Sex as Energy

The way our sexuality functions is not something we ordinarily think much about. Like most of our bodily functions – digestion, breathing and so on – it happens without much conscious awareness. So long as it seems to be working OK, we don't normally pay much attention to the way in which it actually works.

As a result, our experience of sex has a hit and miss unpredictability about it. Sometimes it all comes together, and we have a great time. At other times, all the wheels fall off, and the experience goes nowhere.

We don't really understand why the experience can be so changeable. The magazines try to convince us it is all a matter of technique – yet our experience will show us that technique is no guarantee of sexual satisfaction. The medical profession just wants us to take a pill when things aren't going well. The understanding of the so-called experts in our culture has not proved very helpful.

What is not commonly recognised in our culture's efforts to understand sex is the connection between sex and bioenergy. This is the missing piece of the jigsaw, and our failure to recognise it leads to much of the lack of understanding that still exists about how sex actually works. It is only through recognising this connection, and co-operating with it, that we can make our experience of sex something wonderful and satisfying every time.

An article on women's sexuality in Time magazine stated 'Whether you're male or female, the basic necessities for sexual activity are the same: working sexual anatomy, normal hormone activity and enough physical and mental health to respond to another person'. The first two items – sexual anatomy & hormones

– represent the commonly held wisdom on how our sexuality functions. What the last phrase means is not very clear. It is typical of the kind of fuzzy language often used to cover a lack of understanding of sex.

What is interesting about this statement is that it misses the most vital and central ingredient of our sexuality – its bio-energetic aspect. Without recognising the connection between sex and bioenergy, our understanding remains incomplete, confined to a physical, mechanical view. We see sex as just a set of hormones triggering off physical arousal, which is brought to a climax by friction on the nerve ends in the genital area. What is missing from this picture is the inner experience. The physical act produces certain sensations in the body, which we feel.

The feelings and sensations of sex are the result of bioenergy moving through the body. This energy is something quite different from the hormones and nerve ends. Nerves and hormones can affect the movement of bioenergy – but they are not one and the same thing. The truth of this can be demonstrated very simply by observing the fact that the same physical routine of sex produces very different feelings and sensations at different times. Sex can vary from thrilling all the way to boring. The same hormones and nerve ends are involved, but the inner experience can be very different.

Why is there such a variation in the experience of sex at different times? The authors of the above-mentioned article in Time try to explain this difference by changes that occur in mood, stress levels and so on. This is again using the same fuzzy language that obscures more than it reveals. People who are sensitive to the movement of energy in their bodies invariably report a direct relationship between an *open flow of energy*, and a satisfying and pleasurable experience of sex.

In order to have a clear and realistic understanding of our sexuality, we need to understand the energy that makes it work. This doesn't mean that we need a lot of theoretical knowledge about energy. What we need is very simple – to be able to recognise and experience the movement of energy in the body.

Once we make the connection between energy movement and

sex in our own experience, then everything starts to fall into place. We have an understanding that will enable us to tune in to the true nature of our sexuality, and make the experience of sex thrilling and sensational each time.

What is this energy?

We have introduced the concept of bioenergy in the second chapter. Bioenergy is another term for the life force – it is that which animates us and enables us to move, dance, walk and talk. It is that which gives us a glow of aliveness, a radiance, and a bounce in our step. This life force is found in everything that is alive – plants, insects, animals, even the earth and the atmosphere. If you gaze with soft focus into the space in front of you on a clear sunny day, you will see tiny dots of light dancing haphazardly a short distance before your eyes. These are little pockets of energy. We absorb them into our bodies as we breathe. In fact, breathing, digesting food, and contact with nature are our main sources of energy. This is how our bodies become energised.

This energy then starts to move through the body. It makes its way through the energy pathways of the acupuncture meridians, energising all of the internal organs. We use it up in activity, work, emotions, sex and other ways. As far as understanding our sexuality is concerned, what we need to recognise is the connection between energy movement and sensations in the body.

Energy movement in the body produces different sensations in different places. Energy moving through the muscles produces activity and heat, in the belly it digests the food and produces emotion, and in the genital area it produces sexual sensations.

This is really how our sexuality gets switched on and off. When energy accumulates and starts to move through the sexual area, we feel sexual. When it is not moving in the sexual area, we do not feel sexual. This is the reason why external stimulation of the erogenous zones can sometimes produce no effect – our energy is not ready to move. And sometimes even the mildest stimulus creates a strong response – our energy is ready to move.

Knowing this connection between sexuality and energy helps

us to understand much of what we need to know about how our sexuality functions. If our sexuality is not functioning in a healthy way, understanding the problem in terms of the underlying energetics shows us how we can correct any type of sexual dysfunction. Premature ejaculation and erectile dysfunction in men can be treated very effectively with bioenergetic therapy. Sexual unresponsiveness in women can also be treated in the same way.

I had a client some time ago, Julia, a woman in her mid-twenties, who complained that the experience of sex was 'painful and a waste of time'. She was an attractive woman, educated, and had had many lovers – from one-night stands to several live-in boyfriends. She explained that she liked male company, and put up with sex just to please the men.

Her family was not particularly religious, and there were no indications of guilt or shame in relation to sex. There had not been any abuse, or traumatic experience in her past. She was very fond of her father, but her relationship with her mother was severely strained. She described her mother as being emotionally insecure, and as someone who alternated between being subtly manipulative and overtly controlling with her – in an attempt to get some sort of attention and affection.

The more her mother fell apart emotionally, the more Julia felt the need to be responsible and hold herself together. She became excessively controlled, and developed an aversion to her own feminine nature. These characteristics both emerged in her experience of sex. She found herself being an observer, rather than able to participate in the experience. And her controls had become so ingrained, that it had become impossible for her to let go and surrender to the experience.

To her credit, she had not tried to fake it with her boyfriends. Nor had she tried to get herself turned on by artificial means. In fact, she would say to her lovers 'OK, you have got five minutes', then lie back and time them as they got busy. She had remained true to herself in spite of her problems, and it was this honesty that brought her to therapy – and which, in the end, helped her to overcome her difficulties. It says much for her charm and attractiveness that, in spite of her lack of responsiveness, several of her boyfriends had still wanted to marry her.

The treatment with her was very simple. It was to learn to recognise, accept and surrender to the sensations of sexual energy in her body. We started with some special physical exercises to loosen up the tightness in her body. Then it was a matter of learning to identify sexual sensations, and allow them to move spontaneously through the body. Some affirmations helped to strengthen her acceptance, and overcome the mental aversion she had developed towards sex. Within six to eight weeks she was experiencing multiple orgasms spontaneously.

Some emotional healing was also needed, but her ability to enjoy sex has remained with her.

It is beyond the scope of this book to go into the treatment of sexual disorders in detail. The reader is referred to *Bioenergetics* and other works by Alexander Lowen for more information.

What we will be exploring is how you can make this connection between sexuality and energy in your own experience. As we will see, this is the key to discovering a natural delight in sexuality on a regular basis, and to understanding the connection between sex and the heart.

Maximising Sexual Delight

Why – if sex has worked perfectly OK so far – is it important to start recognising the connection between sexual feelings and energy movement in the body? Of what benefit will this be?

What it will do for you is give you sexual expertise. By knowing and understanding the deepest secrets of sexuality, you will have the ability to maximise the enjoyment of sex, both for yourself and for your partner. This will greatly increase your attractiveness to the opposite sex, and help many of your fantasies and desires to become realised.

If you really look honestly at the way you approach sex, you will recognise that, no matter how exciting it may get at times, it has some limitations. There are times when your sexual experience goes nowhere, and just becomes repetitious and boring. Most people's sexuality is driven by technique and fantasy, which provide only a limited degree of satisfaction.

Making the connection between sexual sensations and energy movements in the body will enable you to maximise not only your own enjoyment of sex, but your partner's also. Your sexual experience will take a quantum leap from being just OK, to being sensational.

How this happens will be explained in the rest of this chapter.

Firstly, let's look at how we can make the connection between sexual sensations and energy movements in the body, within our own experience. This is the key to sexual mastery.

Discovering Your Energy
What we are talking about here is getting out of our heads, and into our bodies. Sexual sensations happen in the body – they are not something we have to think about.

If you are not sure what a sensation is – just slap yourself right now. Make it a hard slap, so there will be no misunderstanding. Assuming that your nervous system is working OK, you will notice that there is a funny, stinging, tingling, smarting sort of feeling occurring in the area you have just slapped. This is a *sensation*. So sensations are not thoughts, or images, or ideas – they are feelings, pure and simple. Feelings and sensations do not occur in the brain. They occur in the body. All we have to do is notice them. We do this by both feeling them, and perceiving the feeling through direct conscious attention.

There are many different types of sensation. Some, such as the one described above, occur as a result of an *external* stimulus. Others occur as a result of an *internal* stimulus. There are no slaps, or bumping of heads, and yet we feel all sorts of things happening inside the body – things like hunger pangs, aches and pains, "butterflies in the stomach', pleasure, the urge to eliminate, and so on. What triggers off these sensations? Where does the stimulus for these sensations come from? These sensations are triggered by the movement of energy inside the body – within the muscles and internal organs.

Rather than being slapped, we are being gently caressed by energy moving around inside us.

It is when this caressing energy movement reaches the genital area that your sensations start to become sexual. You may be sitting around on your own, just reading a book, and suddenly you feel something stirring inside. Even without the presence of a partner, energy can at times start moving through the sexual chakra, caressing and stimulating the very sensitive area of the genitals, and spreading out in waves to the muscles of the pelvic area and beyond. When this happens, resist the urge to start fantasising and daydreaming. Stay with the sensations in the body and just feel them.

You are being touched from the inside! Notice all the different sensations – the tingling, the desire, the softness, the lusciousness, the fire, the passion, the yearning, the aliveness, the sweetness. Words are very inadequate to describe sensations. The word 'passion' and the experience of passion are two totally different things. So as you tune in to the different sensations, don't think about the words – just experience and notice the actual feeling itself, as it occurs within the body.

So far, all of this is happening as the result of an internal stimulus only – the caressing movement of energy passing through the genital area.

Now imagine what happens when an external stimulus is added to this. An external stimulus from someone who is sensitive and caring, and is tuned in to your internal energy movements. It is like oxygen being added to the fire. Your breathing deepens, the sensations in the genital and pelvic area intensify, and the desire arises in you to let go and surrender to this growing wave of energy and sensation.

But something may still hold you back. You may not be sure if you can trust your partner sufficiently to be able to let go. Is he or she really present with you – are they really aware and responsive to your energy movements? Or are they just practicing some technique, or getting lost in their own world? Everything depends on this. When the external stimulus from one's partner is not in tune with our internal energy movements, instead of feeling more pleasure, we start to feel the opposite – a sense of irritation and contraction.

When our partner is not in tune, our sexual experience together will have a hit and miss uncertainty about it. Sometimes we get lucky – the internal and external happen to coincide – and it all works fine. At other times this doesn't happen, and the experience becomes just an irritation.

If our partner has developed a sensitivity and attunement with our internal energy movements, and we can recognise this, a trust develops towards them, and we feel confident about giving in to the urge to let go and surrender. Our resistance melts, and waves of the most exquisite sensations flood through us.

How do we become more sensitive to the movement of energy within ourselves and our partner? It is simply a matter of paying attention, and feeling what is happening inside. Ordinarily, our attention is focussed outside, on the external stimulus – the music, our partner etc. Or else we get lost in our imagination. In either case, we don't pay any attention to what we are feeling inside.

Paying attention to feelings means having a two-way focus. One part of our awareness goes outward, towards our partner. The other part of our awareness moves inwards, tuning in to the feelings in our body. At first this may seem a little awkward, and we need to spend some time developing the habit of a two-way focus. Eventually, it becomes automatic, and we are able to relate to our partner with a great deal more sensitivity and awareness. As we learn to flow with the subtle movements of energy within ourselves and our partner, our sexual activity becomes more and more pleasurable and blissful. This two-way focus leads eventually to a greater sense of oneness between ourselves and our partner during sexual intimacy.

Becoming aware of feelings and sensations in the body also tells us when sexual energy is *not* present. It helps us to overcome habits of indulgence and craving that can debilitate us, and keeps our sexuality more spontaneous, and aligned with its true nature.

We need a natural appetite for something before we can really enjoy it. The person who is hungry relishes their food, whereas someone who overeats does so without much enjoyment. They are merely gratifying a mental craving rather than a bodily appetite. It is the same with sex. When the desire for sex arises spontaneously within the body, the experience has a joy and intensity about it that is missing when we are just indulging.

Learning to discriminate between these two comes from listening to and recognising the wisdom of the body.

The Wisdom of the Body

We live in a culture that is to a large extent head-centred. We have developed a lot of expertise in the areas of technology, intellectual understanding and so on. One result of this is that we have lost an awareness of, and attunement with, the wisdom of the body. Body-wisdom is not something you can get from a book. You get it from listening to your body.

A head-centred person approaches life in a cerebral way. He or she is always figuring out what the best thing to do is in each situation. In matters of business, or choosing a house or a car – in practical matters – this approach is very effective. However, when dealing with the body, it is far less so. For example, when it comes to diet, the mind can get into a lot of confusion trying to figure out what the best diet is to follow. There are so many different and conflicting theories and ideas. The fact is that each individual has different needs at different times. When we listen to the body it will tell us what food is best for us at any time. An imposed diet may be inappropriate for our needs at certain times, and cause us a lot of unnecessary distress and discomfort, but when we follow the wisdom of the body, it always leads to a sense of wellbeing.

The same is true of our sexuality. The body has its own wisdom when it comes to sex. For example, the body will tell you if you are sexually compatible with someone – if there is a sexual chemistry there – or not. You can't manufacture a sexual chemistry that isn't there. By tuning in to, and experiencing, the sensations in the body, your body will reveal to you whether chemistry exists or not.

There are many other things that the wisdom of the body will teach us. Should men be aggressive or gentle? Should women be receptive, or should they take the initiative? Are fantasies OK? When is pornography helpful, and when is it harmful? These are not questions that we can sort out in our heads. The sensations in the body will reveal the answers. If we feel a genuine sense of upliftment from any of these activities, then we know that, in that moment, it is the right thing to do. At another time, that sense of upliftment may be missing. We may, instead, feel ourselves deflated. This is the body telling us that, in this moment, this activity is not right for us. Tuning in to, and surrendering, to the wisdom of the body will always enhance our joy and wellbeing in that moment.

As we start to tune in to, and surrender to the sensation of inner energy movement, we discover a very surprising thing – *our energy is innately intelligent!* We recognise that the energy movement inside the body *knows what it is doing.* By tuning in to it, and following it without interfering, we discover that it always leads us to clarity and wellbeing. By practicing this kind of trust, surrender and let-go in our lives, we soon discover for ourselves how awe-inspiring and intelligent our inner nature is.

Many of us still view our inner nature with mixed feelings. We may have an appreciation for the intricacy of the human body, but we often view our inner world with fear and mistrust.

Our fear comes, as always, from ignorance. We don't understand our inner nature, so we fight with it, trying to control and subdue it. We fail to see the innate beauty, grace and intelligence that is already there.

Nature is performing miracles of intelligent control within us every moment. For example, it maintains our bodies at a constant temperature. Whenever we step outside – moving from a warm to a cold environment – signals pass around the body, adjustments are made to our metabolism, the heart rate picks up, we burn up a little more fat – and our body temperature maintains itself perfectly. It is all done without any fuss or fanfare – yet the body doesn't miss a beat.

We take all these things for granted. We may have been taught about them in school, but often in a dry, mechanistic fashion, using technical terms such as 'homeostasis' to describe these little daily miracles, that we fail to fully appreciate the intelligence behind them. As we start to listen to our inner nature, its beauty and intelligence become more apparent, and we learn to appreciate and trust our body's innate wisdom.

Body-wisdom also shows us how to maximise our enjoyment of sex. When we approach sex in a spontaneous fashion, listening and surrendering to the energy movements in the body, sex loses its fluctuating uncertainty, and is always experienced as a delight.

Having seen that sex is, in addition to its physical elements, an energy movement that causes sensation, and having recognised the wisdom that is innate to our energy system, we are prepared for the next step in returning to the true nature of our sexuality – the art of letting go.

Control and Letting Go

Letting go and surrendering to sexual feelings is an experience that is difficult to describe in words. We can get some sense of this experience by backtracking a little – back to when we were discovering our energy.

As you recall, we were sitting around not doing anything much, when we noticed the first stirring of sensations in the area of the second chakra. Rather than going off into fantasy, we stayed with the feelings, just tuning into them and noticing the various flavours, textures and intensities of each sensation as it arose in the body. Having discovered that sexual sensations are caused by energy moving in the genital area, we may marvel at the wonder of the feeling of the life force moving through us. Now, as we recognise the innate intelligence and in-built ability of our energy system to regulate and control itself, whatever fear or anxiety we may have about allowing these feelings free rein starts to dissolve. We feel ready to accept and experience more of our sexual feelings.

Then an external stimulus, in the form of a caring and sensitive partner, was added to the internal stimulus we were experiencing. Let's suppose that by now we have learnt to trust in them, and we

welcome their touch. We notice all the sensations in our body inten-
sifying. Our partner senses this, and may adjust what they are doing
to enhance and deepen our experience. At the same time, we tune in
to what is happening within them, as we continue to stay present
with the ever-increasing sensations of passion and pleasure that
arise in our body. Both partners start catching the waves of excitement together. We become like surfers riding the waves of passion
on an ocean of ecstasy and delight. Like surfers, we remain poised
and balanced, not allowing the waves to dislodge us. We become
attuned with the surf, sensing the movement of the waves beneath
us, and riding them in a state of contained let go and surrender,
adjusting to the changing flow in each moment. Our bodies become
the ocean, our feelings are the waves and we are both the ecstasy of
the waves and the surfer riding them. As we gain mastery over this
experience, we can deepen and prolong it.

Eventually, as the waves build higher and higher, and start to
approach a climax, we surrender completely, allowing ourselves to
be engulfed by the tumultuous waves of orgasmic bliss as they crash
in a frenzy all around us.

The euphoric stillness of the calm after the storm descends on
us. We find ourselves drifting on a tranquil ocean, being carried
along by much quieter tidal movements. Eventually there is the gentle bump of our body reaching the shore, and the final lapping of
small waves pushing us back onto firm ground.

This is something like the experience that letting go can bring you
to. This kind of experience cannot be brought about by technique.
With technique, rather than allowing feelings of arousal to occur
naturally and spontaneously, we start trying to make them happen.
In other words, we are controlling and manipulating the whole situation, steering it towards some desired goal that we have set in
advance. We are not in tune with our partner, but are just getting lost
in our own world. Our experience of sexuality then becomes superficial and unsatisfying, lacking in the deeper pleasures that spontaneity and letting go can bring, and lacking a sense of genuine, intimate
connection with our partner.

This is what causes a couple to become bored with sex. After a while, you are just repeating the same old mechanical routine. It all becomes a bit ho hum. It's what we might call 'head oriented' sex, i.e. sexual activity that is driven by the idea of sex, rather than by the feeling of sex.

The only remedy for this situation is to become body oriented rather than head oriented. Sexual energy arises in the body, not in the mind. This is where the real juice is, and we turn on the flow of this juice not through control and manipulation, but through relaxing and letting go. We need to understand that our sexual energy will move through us spontaneously by itself. We don't have to try and make it happen.

To make this shift from head to body, there are five steps you need to take:

1. Give up the desire in your mind to control and manipulate the situation. Let the mind be relaxed without thought or expectation. Simply enter the present moment with awareness.

2. Relax and tune in to your body, and feel the actual physical sensations arising within, in the present moment.

3. Accept whatever you feel in each moment. Don't try to make it better, bigger, brighter etc. Let each moment be enough.

4. Breathe into your belly and pelvic area. Connect your breath to the feelings as they arise spontaneously, and let the feelings expand through your body as you breathe out.

5. Surrender to what you are feeling. Tune in to your partner, and allow yourselves to move together so that the feelings in each moment spontaneously become stronger and stronger for both of you. Ride the waves of your energy, enjoying each moment. Learn to contain and sustain more and more pleasure and bliss before reaching a climax.

Sexuality and Technique

From the preceding discussion we can see that technique alone is no guarantee of sexual satisfaction, despite what the magazines might try to tell us. There are times when whatever we are doing happens to coincide with the internal energy movements, and everything is fine. At other times, this doesn't happen, and the experience goes nowhere.

We can avoid this variability by coupling technique with sensitivity to energy movements, both within ourselves and in our partner. This awareness of feeling will help us decide what to do to enhance the energy movements. This means we must be present, and attentive, and tuned in at all times. Energy movement and sensation can change any moment, and only our sensitivity in the moment can direct us where to go next. When we are on the right track, we will feel it – our feelings and sensations will become stronger. So our feelings in the moment become both a feedback of what is happening, and a cue as to where to go next.

Once our partner feels that we are in tune with them, they can relax and start to trust us. This creates the possibility for the deeper sensations of orgasm to arise. The most intensely pleasurable sensations of sexuality can only arise in a deep let go, when we can drop our defences and surrender to the passionate movement of energy within.

This happens not through technique, but through relaxing and letting go – a letting go that is created through trust, both in ourselves and in the other person.

Before this process of letting go and trusting becomes part of a relationship, it may be necessary to communicate to our partner at times when things are not going well. People's egos are often sensitive in this area, so it is best to reach an understanding with your partner that each of you is willing to receive feedback from the other. Without this permission from your partner, feedback is likely to be met with some resistance.

When sexual activity is approached in this way, it ceases to be routine and boring. Each time it is new and different and spontaneous. Because we are not planning and controlling it, but simply riding the waves of energy, we never really know what will happen next. The movement of energy in the body, and the experience of it, is always changing. No matter how many times we make love, our experience of it remains fresh and surprising and new.

Furthermore, as you become more confident and adept at letting go and trusting and surrendering, greater depths of pleasure open up, in ways you could never have imagined. Eventually, your whole body lights up, and the sweetest, most intense sensations of pleasurable energy sweep through you. As you learn to master this energy, the experience of sex can be heightened and prolonged at will. The art of transforming sexual energy into bliss will be discussed in more detail in the second part of this chapter.

Chemistry and Compatibility

The experience of sexual chemistry is familiar to most people. Some people just 'light your fire', while others don't. It may not have a lot to do with their physical appearance, they may not be your 'type', but you feel a strong, magnetic attraction to them.

Sexual chemistry is a result of your sexual energy having a natural vibrational resonance with the other person's. It arises from a combination of astrological, physical, karmic and other factors, over which we have little control. Astrologically, for example, people's sun signs belong to one of four elemental groups – fire, earth, air and water. Each of these elemental energies has a different vibration. A fire sign person will have more chemistry with another fire sign or with an air sign. Earth and water signs are also compatible in the same way. Fire and earth signs are much less compatible, as are fire and water, earth and air, and air and water. This is because air fuels fire, but water puts fire out. Water nourishes earth, but earth smothers fire, and so on. Generally, upward rising signs (fire and air) are compatible, as are downward flowing signs (earth and water).

There are always exceptions to these general rules, and sometimes karmic and other factors will over-ride astrological ones. The only way you can know if you have sexual chemistry with someone is to actually feel it in your body. You will feel an unmistakeable stirring of sensations of attraction in the presence of that person.

If a reasonable degree of sexual chemistry is there between two people, it becomes much easier to surrender to sensations in the body. Your vibrational harmony will actually cause a lot of sensation to be generated between you spontaneously, and you won't have to do much to experience a satisfying sexual connection. If sexual chemistry is low between you, you may find yourself breathing and surrendering and letting go till you are blue in the face – and still nothing much is happening.

Hence the importance of being sensitive to the sensations in your body when you are getting to know someone. You will experience if the chemistry is there or not, and you can chose either to be friends, or to pursue a sexual relationship.

As you become more sensitive to your own energy, you will automatically become more selective about who you chose as a sexual partner. In the context of a loving relationship, the genital area is the gateway to the heart – the roots of the rose bush. We need to be careful who we allow in, because we are absorbing their energy. If their energy is heavy or negative, we take that into ourselves. If you have sex with a lot of different partners, you confuse your energy system with a lot of different vibrational frequencies.

So we may have to give up some of our 'sex as entertainment' options. However, when you find someone compatible and discover the deeper joys that are possible, you'll see that this is no great loss.

Sex and Romance

Once you have met someone compatible on this level, and the attraction is mutual, it is likely that you will fall in love. Falling in love does strange things to people. We start thinking about the other person in an almost obsessive way. We want to be with them all the time. We think they are the most wonderful person on the planet. Everything about them is just so cute and adorable. Maybe he has a dimple on his chin, or you love the way he eats his soup. Whatever it is, we are transported into another world. If there are any hitches to our being together, we are thrown into despair.

It is said that love is blind, and certainly in this state of romantic love, we are temporarily blinded to any of the normal human frailties and shortcomings that our beloved may have. Or if we do see

them we think they are part of their charm. We are convinced that
they are the nearest thing to perfection, that they are 'the one', and
that this feeling of love will last forever. In fact, we are so convinced,
that we start to reschedule our whole future based on this new relationship. We make all sorts of promises and commitments, and are
willing to do whatever it takes to keep this wonderful glow of love
and harmony continuing.

What we don't realise is that we have been drugged by nature.
Romantic love is a bio-chemical trick that nature plays on us, in
order to get us to reproduce. The sexual energy causes certain
chemicals to be released in the brain, namely dopamine and nore-
pinephrine, which are responsible for obsessive thinking and desire.
It's as if nature has slipped some sort of ecstasy drug into our drink,
and is forcing us to find the other person so attractive that we'll be
unable to resist mating with them.

It is the sexual energy causing our brain to go a little haywire.
Falling in love is not really love at all, but is nature's way of getting
us to express our sexual energy, and ensure the continuation of the
species. The proof of this is that once nature has achieved its goal
– once we have mated and (maybe) reproduced – the romantic love
evaporates. The drug wears off, and we are thrown back into our
normal state of perception. We look again at our beloved, and think
'what did I ever see in you? What is that deformity on your chin?
And as for the way you eat your soup, were you raised by wolves?'
Suddenly our perception flips, and all the shortcomings we had been
so oblivious to start appearing before us in sharp focus. In this state
of perception, nature has apparently estimated that the chances of
the human race continuing are severely reduced. So, in its wisdom,
it has created the drug of romantic love.

If you recognise this, a couple of questions may spring to mind.
What to do when you fall in love, and what is love anyway? Let's
look at each of these in turn.

Falling in Love – A Survival Guide
First of all, when you fall in love, accept that it is happening. At the
same time, remain aware that you are under the influence of a pow-

erful bio-chemical change in the brain, which is causing your perceptions to become extremely rose-colored. So don't make any long
term plans or decisions based on your current frame of mind. Stay
in the present moment, and enjoy the ride.

If your partner starts talking about long term commitment, gently discourage them, tell them you need time, and keep them
anchored in the present moment as much as possible.

Ideally, you should refrain from entering into a physical relationship straight away. Take time to get to know the person. Find
out what makes them tick, what their likes and dislikes are, and what
are their aims and aspirations in life. Basically, you want to find out
how compatible you are in other areas of your life, because this is
going to determine whether the relationship has the possibility of
enduring and going deeper.

If you are in love, and the love is not reciprocated, again – accept
that this is happening, and remain aware that there are chemicals
being released in your brain which will cause you to think obses-
sively about the other person. Realise that you will idealise them,
and that your perceptions are being powerfully influenced by your
body's bio-chemistry. The best thing you can do is not co-operate
with these thought processes. Don't give them too much energy or
attention. Watch them in a dis-interested fashion, let them be, and
understand that in time your thought processes will again return to
normal. Simply wait, distract yourself with something interesting,
and let the drug wear itself out.

Highly imaginative people tend to be more strongly swayed by
these kinds of thoughts and feelings. This is because the sexual
energy that fuels romantic love, and the chemicals that accompany
them, trigger off all sorts of romantic dreams and fantasies. There is
a genuinely loving aspect to romantic love, because sex is never just
sex. Sex and love often exist together, and especially so in those with
sensitive natures. Romantic love gives us perhaps our first glimpse
into the possibilities that love has to offer. Free from its obsessiveness and its self-absorption, it can be a window into the joy and
mystery of genuine love. That first glimpse awakens in us the yearn-
ings and longings of the heart. If we can learn to separate fact from

fantasy, it can inspire and motivate us to turn that glimpse into more and more of a reality.

Sex and Love

What is the difference between sex and love? The main difference lies in who we are caring about. In a sexual relationship, we are primarily caring about ourselves. Our concern is mostly for our own pleasure, and our care for the other person is secondary to that, and conditional on whether they satisfy our desires or not. In love, our concern is for the welfare of the other person. Our joy is in giving, and our own wishes and desires are secondary to the wish to see the other happy.

We can sometimes be confused about whether we are in lust or in love, especially if we have fallen in love romantically. These feelings can seem to overlap. Let's look at the connection between them.

Sexual energy is basically self-centred. We want to have sex for our own pleasure, and our partner's attitude is the same. The whole mating dance that precedes sex – the flirting, phone calls, dinners, etc. – is basically a dance of two people thinking about and anticipating their own enjoyment, whether that enjoyment has to do with sex or with romantic love. Once we connect with someone in a sexual relationship, this self-centredness continues. They become 'my partner'. We get possessive and jealous if they show interest in someone else.

Often, we don't want to admit that our interest in the other is basically selfish, and we create all kinds of notions about romantic love. But even romantic love, if you are willing to look at it clearly and honestly, is to a large extent self-centred. The other is essentially seen as an object, either the object of my sexual desire, or my romantic desire or both.

Genuine love is very different from this. It has little to do with 'romance', passion, demands, expectations, possessiveness, commitment, attachment, dependence and all the other emotional states that have been masquerading as love in our lives so far. Love is something quite rare and takes time to cultivate. It is essentially the feeling and attitude of wanting to place the happiness of our beloved ahead of our own. We are not thinking about what we want to get from them. We do not see the other as someone who is there to make us happy, along with all the demands and expectations that accompany this attitude. We see the other as simply precious, beautiful, endearing, and there is a spontaneous feeling of wanting to do whatever we can to ensure that they are happy, without regard for ourselves. In fact, our happiness comes from being able to give to them, just for the joy of giving.

If you look honestly at the feelings of romantic love, you will see that, although there may be some degree of genuine concern for the other, it is mixed with a large amount of self interest.

Sex and love are thus at opposite ends of the spectrum of self interest. Where we are on this spectrum will vary from person to person. We are rarely completely at one end or the other. Usually, we find ourselves at some point along it, with self interest and selflessness mixed in various proportions. Only honest self reflection will reveal to you where you are at any time.

Anyone who has lived through one or more sexual or romantic relationships will start to recognise their limitations. Romance begins feverishly and fades after some time. Sex is pleasurable for a few moments, but there is no deeper joy or love there. Those moments soon pass, and what is left? At least another twenty three and a half hours of your day. Relationships based on sex and romance tend to deteriorate into struggles for possession and battles for control. To an aware and sensitive soul, this situation soon becomes unsatisfactory, and a longing for a more fulfilling, loving relationship starts to arise in the heart.

How to move from sex to love is essentially what the rest of this book is about. The journey from sex to love is probably the most fascinating and rewarding journey any human being can undertake. There are challenges to face, obstacles to overcome, unconscious habits to be made conscious and fears to be conquered. We need to be both a lover and a warrior on this journey, combining sensitivity and strength. It takes courage to move beyond our conditioned habits and cultural norms.

A sincere honesty is one of the main requirements for this journey. In many ways, the journey is a quest for truth – and honesty, especially with oneself, is the one quality that will facilitate the journey more than any other.

If we are honest with ourselves, we will recognise that our sexual attraction to someone has a shadow side. It creates feelings of jealousy and possessiveness, both in ourselves and in our partner. These feelings will often undermine our attempts at creating a loving connection with that person, and may even lead to a relationship based on hostility, fear and mistrust. It is clear that we will need to find some way of overcoming and transforming these negative feelings, if our sexual attraction is to lead to a genuinely loving connection.

Overcoming Jealousy and Possessiveness

To move sexual energy upwards towards the higher chakras, there are some initial obstacles that need to be overcome, relating to the dark side of sexuality. Sex is not just all fun and enjoyment. Because it is so pleasurable, and because this pleasure is entirely dependant on the other person being co-operative, and furthermore, because the sex drive is basically self centred, we start wanting to possess and control the other person. We want them to be there for us, at our disposal, all the time. Possessiveness means we have turned the other from a person into an object. They are not there for themselves. They are there for us. If you have been on the receiving end of this experience, you will know how unpleasant and demeaning it is.

Coupled with possessiveness and the desire to control, there is the frailness of the human ego. Once we have declared our attraction for someone, it places us in a vulnerable position with them. They have the power to accept or reject us. Even if they accept us initially, they may reject us at any time after that. When they start showing an interest in someone else, the possibility of their rejecting us suddenly arises. It brings up in us all of our latent insecurities and fears of rejection. All our doubts about our own attractiveness start to haunt us. This is when the Green Goddess of jealousy becomes our constant companion. Depending on our own sense of security and self esteem, we will be tormented by feelings of worthlessness and anguish and self doubt. Our pain and anger may be so great that we start thinking of revenge. Sexual jealousy has probably driven more people to murder than any other emotion.

The bad news is, if you are human, you will experience these feelings. We don't consciously choose to be this way. These feelings arise instinctively. Sexually possessive instincts are part of our animal nature, and you only need to watch a few documentaries on animal behaviour to see how possessive those people are.

What these documentaries show is mostly the males fighting each other, sometimes to the death, for the right to mate with the females of their choice. The females, meanwhile, are just standing around waiting to see what will happen. They are not interested in fighting or dominating anyone. They seem to be happy to share whoever the dominant male is with their sisters. Innately, males are more possessive and jealous than females.

What sets humans apart from animals is the size of our brain. We are capable of far greater intelligence, yet we rarely make full use of this capacity. As far as sexual and emotional intelligence is concerned, a lot of men are still scraping their knuckles on the pavement. We live in a male dominated society, and many of the sexual norms of our society are created by men. Men are competitive by nature, whereas women are more co-operative and inclusive. There is anthropological evidence to suggest that, in matriarchal societies, feelings of possessiveness and jealousy are far less prevalent, as is monogamy.

Unfortunately, women have become as infected with the emotions of jealousy and possessiveness as men are, but for somewhat different reasons. Through the traditional marriage structure, men have forced women to be dependant on them for survival for many centuries. Till recently, women's emotions of possessiveness and jealousy were not based on sexuality, but on their insecurity about survival. Even though women have liberated themselves from this old bondage, the idea of dependence on a man for security is something that still lurks in the basement of the female psyche. Add to this the fact that women have become very conscious of, and uncertain about, the attractiveness of their appearance, and we now have a situation where, in terms of jealousy and possessiveness, true equality exists between men and women.

The good news is that we humans have the possibility of overcoming these emotions.

How can these emotions be overcome? The key to overcoming all negative emotions is found in the following four steps:

1. Don't *blame*
2. *Acknowledge* and take responsibility for the feeling
3. *Accept* the feeling
4. *Watch* the feeling

When we feel hurt in a relationship our automatic response is often to blame the other person. We believe that if they really cared about us, they wouldn't do anything to hurt us. This is considered to be true at all times and for all situations. The reality is that, while there is some truth in it, it is not the whole story. It is reasonable to expect a degree of sensitivity and concern for our feelings from our partner. Yet we cannot expect them to sacrifice their lives just to keep us feeling good. We must be willing to respect their freedom to be themselves and to follow their own destiny. And if that destiny takes them away from us – temporarily or permanently – we must be willing to accept that, even if it hurts. So before doing anything, we should assess honestly – are they acting selfishly and insensitively? Or are they legitimately following what is right for them? In the first case, we can let them know how it makes us feel. In the second case, we should let them be, and deal with our own hurt by taking responsibility for it.

How do we deal with pain? Our tendency on experiencing a negative feeling is to try to do something about it. We want to change it, be rid of it, make it go away, anything to avoid feeling it. We imagine if we can think the right thoughts, be positive, or analyse the situation, then we can change the way we feel. All of these efforts are futile, and generally just tie us up in knots. We may then try to distract ourselves, or if the feeling is very painful, we drown our sorrows, bury ourselves in work, or try to rebound with someone else. This also doesn't work.

The only thing that works is – don't do anything. Instead of trying to change the feeling, or run away from it – acknowledge and accept it. Be with it. Run towards it, not away from it. It may be painful, but by simply accepting it, it turns out to be far less painful than the knots we tie ourselves up in, trying to avoid it. Breathe into the feeling, and allow it to move through your body. Don't resist it, just let it be there.

At the same time, become a watcher. As the feeling moves through you, let one part of you just observe it, in a detached kind of a way. Don't be identified with it. Just say to yourself, 'pain is happening, and I am watching it'. And let the pain run its course. Eventually, in this way, the pain will subside by itself, and you will be free of it. (see Chapter 6 for more on dealing with pain)

When you have a handle on the pain, start to visualise the situation that is causing it. Don't think about it, just watch the image – maybe your partner with someone else – and feel your feelings. Keep breathing, feeling and watching. More feelings may arise. Allow them to also run their course till they subside. If you can resist thinking about and analysing the situation, then new insights and a new awareness about it may arise spontaneously in you.

I had a client recently whose partner had been unfaithful, and together we went through the above procedure. When her pain and anger had subsided, she continued to visualise her partner together with his new woman, and suddenly she burst out into fits of belly laughter at the ridiculousness of what they were doing, and the absurdity of her jealousy. Actually seeing her partner humping away with this woman was such an absurd image, it just cracked her up. In that moment she became free of all her jealousy.

This is what witnessing can do for us. It is the witnessing consciousness that contains our real intelligence, not our intellect. By giving up thinking and analysing, and switching to witnessing, our intelligence starts to function, and surprising insights arise in us, out of the blue.

The witnessing consciousness also brings light into the situation, and our negative emotions can only exist in the dark. Light illuminates all that is positive, and dispels all that is negative. Jealousy and possessiveness are negative emotions that are part of our animal nature, and arise only when we are unconscious. This means we have not taken the time to observe them, watch them, and see clearly how foolish and destructive they are. Not only that, we have not brought the light of our intrinsic intelligence to bear on them. As soon as we do this, these negative emotions dissolve of their own accord.

It may be difficult to imagine how this can happen if you have never tried it. So all I can suggest is to try it and see what happens. Genuine reflective witnessing *is intelligence in action.* It is shining a light into your darkness. Jealousy and possessiveness only have power over you when you *don't* do this. As soon as you start to watch them, they vanish like darkness in the presence of a candle.

Once we have started to shift some of our negative emotional reactions of jealousy and possessiveness, we can further help ourselves to overcome these tendencies by changing our conditioned thinking. Become aware of your thoughts of jealousy and possessiveness, and recognise that they are destructive to the love you want to create, and make a decision to give them up. When you notice these thoughts arising in you, don't give them any attention. Instead deliberately counter them with affirmations about recognising and honouring the freedom and autonomy of your partner, even if such honouring causes you some pain. Recognise that love can only arise in freedom, and as well as giving that freedom to your partner, also claim it for yourself.

Overcoming these obstacles will smooth the path from sex to love, and remove the negative emotions that interfere with love.

These are the seven steps that will return us to a state of naturalness with our sexuality. To summarise: By recognising sex as energy, by letting go and trusting in the spontaneous movement of that energy in our body with someone compatible, and by avoiding the pitfalls of romantic attachment, jealousy and possessiveness, we align ourselves with the true nature of our sexuality.

This is enough to create a healthy rosebush, which will produce many beautiful blossoms. We are, however, still at the mercy of the forces of nature. In nature, a rosebush will only flower seasonally.

Blossoms come and go, and at times the bush is barren. Nature's agenda is to reproduce. Its purpose is biological, and it has little interest in our spiritual aspirations. There is a way in which we can improve on nature, and create blossoms all year round. This involves transforming our sexual energy into bliss.

In the second part of this chapter we will consider how this can be done.

Part 2. Transformation

Transforming Sexual Energy into Bliss – the icing on the cake

You may have seen photos of ancient Tantric temples in India, now partly ruined, with dozens of statues graphically displaying couples in all sorts of sexual embraces. This is a depiction of the transformation process in action. These temples are offerings to the gods Shiva and Shakti. They show the male and female principles, Shiva and Shakti, coming together in divine union. They are a celebration of sexuality as the source of love and divinity.

If you wish to make this transformation process happen for you, you firstly need to recognise the connection between sex and energy. The connection has been described above, but it needs to be recognised not just as an intellectual understanding, but as a felt experience in your body.

The sexual energy also needs to be liberated. Any fear, guilt or other inhibitions you may have about experiencing sexual energy need to be dropped. Allow yourself to be sexually free. If there are inhibitions that are difficult to overcome, then some affirmations may be helpful. Try the following:

- I give up all negative thoughts about my body and my sexuality
- I now fully embrace and feel all of my sexual energy and sensations

- I celebrate my sexuality totally and freely
- I surrender to the spontaneous arising of sexual passion within me
- I love and relish my sexuality
- I enjoy sharing my sexual energy with my partner
- I surrender without fear or guilt to the joyful explosion of orgasmic delight
- I recognise my sexual energy as the source of love and divinity
- My sexuality opens the doorway to love
- My sexuality opens the doorway to the divine
- I love my body as the temple of the divine

It may seem like a contradiction that in order to create the selfless energy of love, we are creating more of the selfish energy of sex. Most religious and spiritual teachings advise the opposite. The teaching in both Christianity and Buddhism is to suppress sexuality and focus on love, charity and compassion. There is a fear that if too much sexuality is awakened, we will get lost in indulgence and self-centred hedonism. Sex is seen as an enemy to be avoided, rather than as a friend to be embraced.

What these traditional teachings have failed to understand is that sex is everybody's basic nature, and by suppressing it, you are suppressing and condemning a part of yourself. Rather than loving yourself, you end up in conflict with yourself. Sexual desire starts to haunt you, creating guilt and self-loathing. A person in conflict like this, who hates a part of themselves, will find it difficult to love anybody else. Their attempts at love will often have a sense of strain and pretence about them.

Tantra starts with you from where you are. It accepts the reality of you as a sexual being, and celebrates it. There is a deep wisdom in this, because it is only through accepting *what is*, that your heart starts to open. You are not closing down a part of yourself, creating a split between your lower and higher self. Sex is neither beautiful nor ugly – it simply is. When we accept it as it is, with an open heart, a link is created between our sexuality and our heart. The sap of sexuality starts rising up the rosebush, and blossoms begin to appear out of season. Sexual energy is the life force, and as soon as we say 'I love sex', we are saying 'I love life, I love myself, I love my body, I love being alive'. This unconditional self-love makes it easier to accept and love others.

Modern psychology supports this ancient Tantric understanding. Freud, Jung, Reich and others have all pointed to the harmful effects of sexual suppression. It is also now widely recognised that we must love ourselves before we can share love with someone else. And the first step to self-love is to accept ourselves as we are.

In accepting ourselves as we are, we are not 'creating more of the selfish energy of sex' – we are simply recognising and acknowledging the fact that sexual energy is there in us. It is not an exercise in indulgence, but one of self-acceptance and self-love.

The difference between indulgence and Tantra is that indulgence takes sexual activity as an end in itself, whereas Tantra takes sexual activity as a starting point. For Tantra, sex is the beginning but not the end. The Tantric view is that getting the sap moving in the roots of the rosebush might be fun, but the real joy comes from seeing the blossoms appearing. Nobody is going to come and admire the roots of your rosebush. The understanding is that sexuality gives joy and bliss at first, but eventually just sex in itself is not satisfying for most people. There is a greater joy in sharing love, and Tantra has found a way in which sexuality can take us there.

Tantric Sex

The Tantric way to transform sex into love and consciousness makes the spiritual path one of celebration rather than a painful struggle.

To start with, there needs to be an unconditional 'yes' to your sexuality, and a clear recognition that sex is an energy that moves in the body, starting from the second chakra – the genital and pelvic areas.

Then, when you are ready to make love to your partner, it helps to create an atmosphere that is conducive to transforming your sexual energy into something sacred. Take some time to prepare yourself. Set the mood with soft sensual music, and maybe some candles

and incense. Take time to get tuned in to each other, maybe by giving each other a massage first.

Eventually, when the bodies come together, and energy is awakened in the second chakra during lovemaking, it creates a pressure
inside. Energy starts building and it wants to go somewhere. What
normally happens is that it builds to a peak, and is then discharged
in orgasmic release. This is followed by relaxation and a loss of
energy. One becomes tired and wants to fall asleep. This is nature's
rhythm. Orgasmic release, for both men and women (for women it
is the clitoral orgasm), happens through a downward and outward
release of energy. The energy leaves the body and is lost. That is
why one becomes tired and loses interest in one's partner after
orgasmic release.

There is another possibility, which is not commonly recognised
or explored. This is the Tantric practice of retaining the energy
inside the body, and allowing it to move upwards rather than down-
wards. Rather than being lost, it is retained within the body and
allowed to move up towards the heart. As the energy reaches the
heart, it awakens that chakra and all the possibilities of love and joy
contained there.

Sex has been condemned by most spiritual traditions because
they were unaware of this second possibility. With the loss of energy
through orgasmic release, sex leads to a debilitated and low-energy
state, which is unsuitable for spiritual practice. However, the alterna-
tive proposed by traditional religions – to suppress sexual desire –
has proved to be equally harmful. Sex should neither be indulged
nor condemned.

Tantra shows how we can avoid both these pitfalls and use sex
in a way that enhances and enriches spiritual practice. By retaining
the energy within the body, and allowing it to move up to the heart,
the energy is transformed. As sexual energy reaches to and perme-
ates the area of the heart chakra, its vibrational resonance is changed,
and it is felt as love.

How can this change of direction of sexual energy be brought
about? To make this happen, two things are required. Firstly, there
needs to be some sexual discipline, especially on the part of the

male. As the sexual energy, and sexual pressure, builds up in the second chakra during intercourse, the male needs to resist the automatic urge to ejaculate. This is something one can only learn through practice, by trial and error. It need not be attempted through a lot of tension and struggle, but can be done in a relaxed way, with the firmness of one's intention being the main source of one's discipline. The female should also give up all desire to release sexual pressure through clitoral orgasm, and assist the male in maintaining his discipline by helping to keep his arousal within the point of no return. As the sexual energy of each partner becomes more intense, rather than bringing it to a peak, the couple should relax together, and let the energies melt and merge.

Secondly, the upward channel to the heart needs to be cleared of blocks and obstructions within both partners, so that the energy can flow upwards easily. If the energy is able to flow upwards easily, without obstruction, it becomes so much easier to practice ejaculation control, because the sexual pressure no longer just builds up in the second chakra, but can instead be released upwards. If this channel remains blocked, then ejaculation becomes almost inevitable.

How to clear this upward channel to the heart is the subject of the next two chapters.

Transforming sexual energy is the esoteric secret to creating love in abundance. By applying this understanding to your life, you will discover a sense of aliveness, joy, love and bliss that you could not previously have imagined.

Conscious Sexuality

The difference between Tantric and normal sexuality is that one is approached consciously while the other is not. In normal sexuality, we are simply allowing the unconscious forces of nature to take their course. Sexual energy builds up and is released. Some of it moves upwards and reaches to the heart, but much of it is lost. In Tantric sexuality, we are becoming conscious of this natural pattern, and deliberately preventing the release, because we realise that the release depletes us.

To do this, we must make a mental shift from being goal-oriented in sex – i.e. making sexual orgasm the goal – to simply being present in the moment. To be present in the moment, the thinking activity of the mind is not involved. Only our conscious awareness is involved. We direct our conscious attention to the sexual sensations in the body, and just relax and enjoy the experience for its own sake. We are not directing the experience towards a goal, but simply savouring and relishing the changing sensations as they arise and move. Sex becomes a meditation, and we anchor ourselves in the present by becoming a witness to the sensations in the body. At the same time, we create an opening within ourselves for the energy and sensations to move upwards in the body, towards the heart and further up to the head. The act of witnessing has the effect of automatically drawing the energy upwards.

As we relax and surrender to the increasing depth and intensity of the sensations, our bodies become flooded with a greater pleasure and an expanding sense of joy and bliss that creates the possibility for a different type of orgasm altogether. Instead of the normal peak orgasm that is followed by depletion, we enter the Tantric valley orgasm. This is a deeply relaxed state in which we are flooded with blissful energy. It is a state that is tremendously energising and refreshing, and which can be prolonged at will. It is possible for women to experience multiple vaginal orgasms in this state, and even if a man were to occasionally ejaculate in this state, his energy would not be depleted.

So Tantric sexuality is an approach that is not opposed to love and spirituality, but which supports and enhances them. We are not creating a split between sex and love, or between the profane and the sacred, but are creating an inner unity in which sex, love and spirit become integrated into a blissful and orgasmic whole.

Male and Female Sexuality

Most of the preceding discussion can be applied equally to men and women. There are however some differences in the sexual responses of men and women that need to be understood. Women tend to open up sexually as a result of feeling connected to their partner. Men tend to start with sexual attraction, and their feeling of connection comes later, as a result of being sexual. In other words, the initial impetus for a woman comes through the heart, and sexuality follows from there, whereas for a man the initial impetus comes from feeling sexual attraction, and the heart connection follows from there.

So, for a couple to get in sync, it is important for the man to slow down a little, and just be present. He needs to tune in to and feel his energy, and his connection with his partner, without doing anything. In other words, to be patient and wait till she is ready, allowing her to take as much time as she wants. This kind of relaxed, patient, present-in-the-moment connectedness is what really gets a woman going, and he will find that just by doing this, he wont have to wait very long.

(There will be times when an unresolved issue or conflict between both partners interferes with their sense of being connected. Sex is often a barometer for what is happening in other areas of the relationship. When this happens, it is best to take some time out to reflect on the issue, especially on your side of it, and openly share with your partner what is going on. The issue may need to be resolved before your sense of connection can be restored. This process of clearing issues is discussed in the remaining chapters.)

Once the bodies come together, and you have become sensitive to the energy movements, the needs of both partners can be met by allowing your energies to form a circle. Both of you can visualise and feel the following:

As sexual energy is generated in the male, it is allowed to flow and pass into the female at the genital area. She receives the energy into her body, and allows it to move up to her heart. From the heart she gives the energy back to the male, who opens his heart to receive it. He allows the energy to pass down his body to the genital area, and again lets it flow into the woman's body, creating a circle of energy that passes from one to the other. All of this should be done in a relaxed yet energised way, without the male ejaculating. This circle connects the heart and the sexuality of both partners.

Alternatively, both can allow the sexual energy to rise upwards, from the genital area to the heart, and higher.

Sexual Liberation – the next step

We are fortunate to be living in a time when we have so much sexual freedom. We cannot even imagine the kind of frustration that our grandparents must have gone through as a result of the sexual inhibitions and restrictions they had to endure. It is up to us, collectively, to take this liberation one step further, and put sexuality into its right and natural perspective. Not just as something to be indulged in, but as the basis for a loving relationship.

Both as individuals, and as a culture, we are always growing and evolving. The journey is never at an end. The next step for us is to liberate our sexual energy from its present role as a source of entertainment, and realise its potential to bring awakening to the energies of the heart.

As our energies start to move upwards to the heart, the first potential barrier they encounter is the one at the solar plexus. In the next chapter we will explore how to keep the channel open at the third chakra. This unblocking and opening of the upward channel is necessary whether we are following a natural sexuality, or practicing Tantra. In both cases, energy wants to move upwards towards the heart. The only difference is one of degree – with natural sexuality there is less energy available to move up. In all other respects, clearing the way at the power centre is necessary for everyone who is endeavouring to cultivate more love in their lives.

Chapter 5

Power

Most couples can remember their first argument. That turning point in a relationship when the romantic glow suddenly started to dim, and a different energy entered – the energy of conflict. What is striking and amusing about first arguments is that they are often about something totally trivial. I can remember arguing with a past girlfriend about whose turn it was to go out and buy the milk. We were very much in love, and everything was just great, but we had run out of milk. I expected her to go out and buy some, which she normally did. For some reason, on this occasion, she didn't want to go. I had prepared the breakfast that morning, and was busy with some work. I didn't want to go either. I tried to persuade her to go. She refused, saying I was the one who used most of the milk anyway. The tone of the conversation went from friendly, to strained, to heated. We were both convinced that the other person should be the one getting the milk. We ended up with both of us in a bad mood for the rest of the day – and no milk.

Our relationship had moved from the second to the third chakra – from the 'being in love' stage to the 'struggle for control' stage. According to current relationship theory, relationships progress through 3 stages – from dependence to independence to interdependence.

The first stage, dependence, represents the attraction and 'falling in love' stage of the *sexual chakra*. It is characterised by the mutual desire to be in each other's company, and the sense of dependence that that creates. The second stage, independence, represents the struggle for control of the *power chakra*. It is a reaction to the dependency of the first stage, and is characterised by a desire to re-assert control and independence. The third stage, interdependence, represents the acceptance and mutual regard of the *heart chakra*. I doubt that the author of this theory had any awareness of the chakras, however these three stages mirror almost exactly the progression of a relationship through the chakras.

Once the first romantic flush wears itself out, a new energy enters the relationship – the energy of the power chakra. Most relationships fall apart at this stage. No matter how understanding, mature and tolerant we may be in other relationships, in a relationship based on sexual attraction we come up against all of our unconscious power and control issues. We may be a wonderful friend or a great brother or sister, and yet find ourselves turning into a complete control freak with our sexual partner. This is because with friends the dynamic of sexual attraction is not there, and there is no sexual energy starting to move up and hammer away at the power chakra.

In this chapter we will explore the workings of the power chakra, and see how we can negotiate our way through the roadblocks and minefields contained here.

Understanding the Power Chakra

The energy of the power chakra has to do with what we want. As we saw in Chapter 2, the statement at this chakra is 'I Want'. Personal power is about making choices. It is about knowing who you are and what you want. It is about taking control of your life and being courageous enough to go after what you want.

How do we know what we want? Often we are not clear about what choice to make, or we want things that are not in harmony with who we are – our true nature.

Our 'wants' may be divided into three categories:
1. What we have been brought up to want
2. What our ego wants
3. What we really want

Usually these three groups of wants are all mixed up together in our minds, and we start asking or expecting or demanding things from our partner that are unrealistic, unclear, not true to ourselves, egoistic and – occasionally – that which we really do want. Our partner will be doing the same with us.

It is not difficult to sort out our conditioned and ego 'wants' from our real wants. *Our real wants will give us joy, whereas our conditioned wants will just bring misery and unhappiness.* That is why the third chakra is also sometimes called the emotional chakra, because it is our emotional responses of joy and sorrow that confirm whether our choices are good for us or not. Personal power and emotion are closely related in this way.

To do this, we need to be in touch with our emotions, and to be able to distinguish between real joy and the fleeting pleasure of pleasing our parents or satisfying our ego.

Wants are Individual

What we want is a very individual thing. Some people want to be rich, while others have little interest in money. Some people are very interested in sex, while others are far less so. Some pursue positions of power while others are indifferent to it. For some people, love is the most important thing in life, while for others fame and fortune are far more attractive. There are those whose whole passion is to be creative – to paint, or write or act, while many have little time for creative pursuits. Finally, there are a few people whose main goal is spiritual awakening, while for many others this is a matter of complete indifference.

How do we account for these differences in people? Why is someone a business executive while his brother may be a spiritual seeker? I believe that each of us is, in essence, a soul moving towards divine awakening. We are each at different stages of this journey. There are older and younger souls, and souls with negative karma that needs to be cleared. The journey may take many lifetimes to complete.

The journey itself can be compared to the map of the seven chakras. It is a journey from our unconscious, animal nature to a discovery of our divine nature, and consists of seven broad stages that are represented by the seven chakras.

When a soul incarnates into a human body, it brings with it the memories, imprints, experiences, lessons, karmas, and desires of its previous lives. Depending on how many past lives a soul has had, it will have discovered both the joys and limitations of money, sex, power, and/or love etc. If it failed to earn enough money in its previous life, it will bring with it a great desire to make money. Money will be its desire and joy – until it has enough money to begin to experience the limitations of money. Then the desire and appeal of money will diminish, and the energy will move to the second chakra. A new desire will arise – the desire for sex. Rather than money, it is now sex that the soul sees as its source of joy. It may be too old to fulfil this desire in the same lifetime, and will end its life with an unfulfilled desire and longing for sex. It brings that desire with it into its next life, and rather than chasing money, will start to chase sexual experiences. It may take a considerable time for the incarnated soul to attract and explore enough sexual partners before it comes to the recognition that sexual joy is also limited. It then starts to lose interest in sex, and may develop an interest in power, or love.

The soul's progress is usually not a linear one. Some souls start with power, and if they haven't completed their lessons with money, may become prone to financial corruption which their position of power opens them to. This may create a negative karma and cause them reincarnate into a life of poverty, or become a victim of abuse of power. Other souls are very developed at the third eye chakra but may be clueless when it comes to sexuality – and so on. In reality, we can zigzag from one chakra to another until the basic lessons of each chakra are learnt.

What all this means is that the choices we make, and hence what gives us joy, will vary from individual to individual, depending on where we are on our soul's journey.

Recognising Where You Are

You will recognise where you are by honestly acknowledging what it is that gives you joy. The soul reveals its true desires to you through the imagination. So your imagination will become fired up by thoughts of wealth, or sexual pleasure, or power, or love etc. This will become your 'dream' – your deepest inner longing.

At the same time, there may be other factors trying to influence the choices you make. Our family and social conditioning may disapprove of our 'dream', and try to force us to follow a way of life which others believe is best. It may be that our parents want us to have a secure career, while we want to be creative – to paint, or write, or act etc. We may become confused about what choices to make.

This confusion can be clarified by using our imagination. If the image of a secure career fills you with joy, then this is the right choice for you. However, if it fills you with a sense of boredom and dread, then you should take a decisive stand against it, and choose to follow your own dream instead. This is where our sense of being personally empowered takes on great importance.

Becoming Empowered

Far too often, people give away their power. One of the biggest fears we have is the fear of the opinion of others. "What will others think?" is what really inhibits many people from following their dream. There is often a struggle within each person between wanting to be liked and being true to themselves.

Personal power enables you to stand up to others and resist their attempts to control and influence you. Personal power enables you to state "this is what I want', and stick to your guns.

Once you are clear about what you want, you should never be embarrassed or apologetic about it. You are here on this earth to fulfil your soul's purpose. Life will always support you in fulfilling your purpose, even if certain individuals do not. It is far better to give up the support of one or two individuals, and take on the support of life and the universe. The universe is infinitely more powerful, and will be a far greater ally to you, than any group of individuals.

We have talked about overcoming fear through courage and trust in a previous chapter. These are the qualities that help to empower us to stand up and say 'this is what I want'.

Empowerment and Relationships

A relationship is two individuals coming together. Each will have their own dreams, desires, wants and soul's purpose. They will also have their conditioned wants and expectations. For a relationship between two people to have a chance of making it beyond the third chakra, there are three things that the individuals in the relationship need to do.

1. To become clear within themselves of the difference between their conditioned wants and their real wants
2. To communicate their real wants to their partner
3. To listen to, respect and accept the real wants of their partner

It is in the failure of couples to follow each of these three steps that most relationships get bogged down and fall apart.

The result of this kind of communication is that each person in the relationship knows exactly where they stand. It becomes clear whether the two people have enough interests and aspirations in common to enable the relationship to continue in a harmonious and mutually satisfying way.

If the couple don't have enough aspirations in common, then they will probably choose to separate, or become friends.

Instead of following these steps, what usually happens is that we try to influence the other to follow our dream. It is not just that others are trying to influence us. We are also trying to influence them, and we do this mostly within our personal relationships. This is an unhealthy use of power, and is destructive to our personal relationships.

Let's say, for example, that one person in a relationship wants to have children and the other doesn't. Let's also suppose that to each person it is clear that this is a real want. Both will end up trying to persuade the other the give up *their* want. There will be arguments, debates – a power struggle will ensue within the relationship.

Each person is attached to keeping the relationship, and to having their wants and dreams. It is clear that for one of them, both are not possible. Yet each is determined that they will not be the one missing out. They are also most likely convinced that, if the other person really loved them, they would grant them their wish. The other person appears to be behaving very selfishly and inconsiderately.

This kind of power struggle can go on for many years. It usually ends in a stalemate, or with one party giving in, or with the relationship falling apart.

Power struggles of this nature happen when the energy of power is being used unconsciously. The desire for power, control and influence exists in all of us, and comes from the energy of the third chakra. Just as sexual energy when used unconsciously leads to depletion and lethargy, so power used unconsciously leads to a negative and destructive state.

In addition to the real wants that exist at the deeper level of each person, there are our daily wants. These may be called our likes and preferences – such as how to decorate the house, what movie or restaurant to go to, and so on. These can also be the subject of argument and disagreement. How we deal with these issues also reveals to us something about how we deal with power and control issues in a relationship. Most of these kind of disagreements can be resolved with some goodwill, commonsense and flexibility on both sides.

The Healthy Use of Power

To use power in a healthy way, we must avoid the extremes of being either a doormat or a control freak. In other words we must freely express our real wants to our partner, and acknowledge and respect our partner's real wants.

If our wants clash, or are mutually exclusive (one wants children and the other doesn't), we must be intelligent enough to see that the relationship is not the right one for us, and give it up. We must be willing to love in a non-possessive way. We must recognise that our real wants (i.e. our soul's purpose) are more important than the relationship, i.e. fulfilling our real wants will bring us more joy than hanging on to an unfulfilling relationship. And that life will support us in our real wants, but an unfulfilling relationship will most likely fall apart anyway.

There will be other situations where the difference between each person's wants is not so great as to be mutually exclusive. For example, one person may have a career or interest that takes them away for certain periods. If we recognise that this is a real want of theirs, we should be willing to support them. Where there are grey areas, we should give up our demands and expectations for a 'perfect' relationship, and willingly support our partner in their pursuit of their soul's purpose.

Sorting all this out takes time and patience and skill. Neither partner will always be clear about what their conditioned wants are, and what their real wants are. Sometimes we only learn how to discriminate within a relationship, through trial and error. This can be a bumpy and at times painful process. The work that each person has to go through in understanding and clearing the power chakra is often a part of the relationship itself. None of us comes into a relationship in an ideal state. A big part of each relationship is that it is an occasion for each partner to learn some valuable lessons.

If you have tendencies to give your power away, then a big lesson for you will be to learn to stand up and express your real wants, and not allow yourself to be persuaded to give them up. If, on the other hand, you have tendencies to being overly controlling and dominating, your lesson will be learning to listen to your partner and to acknowledge and respect their real wants, without trying to impose your agenda.

These lessons don't come easily to most people. Thrashing them out is all part of the journey of being and growing together.

Healthy Fighting

One of the quickest ways to learn these lessons is through fighting. Sometimes it is good to have a fight. Not physically, but verbally. It clears the air. It improves the circulation, which is good for the skin. Mostly it shakes things up and brings some spark and fire into the relationship. A few heated words can hit closer to the bone than a thousand hours of rational analysis.

We are all human. None of us is perfect. In addition to being wonderful, we do silly things sometimes. We get all puffed up with ego, we make absurd and unfair demands on our partner. We can get irritated with people for all sorts of reasons – some valid, some less so.

I am not saying that fighting is a necessity, but if the energy of irritation is building up, it is better to let it out than to hold on to it. No matter how much we may love someone, there are times when we will be angry with them, or even hate them. A psychologically healthy relationship makes allowances for these times. It shows we are not indifferent, we care passionately, we are engaged with the other person at all levels.

To avoid inflicting too much harm on the relationship, there are certain ground rules in a verbal confrontation that ought to be followed. Firstly, as much as possible, avoid blaming and pointing the finger. Make 'I' statements i.e. statements about yourself, which include your feelings.

For example, "I am angry/hurt about......"

"I hate it when ...."

This lets the other person know how *their* behaviour makes *you* feel. They are less likely to feel criticised or under attack, and hence less likely to feel the need to defend themselves.

Also, advice giving is generally not helpful. It is not your job to fix the other person up. They have not come to you for therapy or spiritual guidance. It is up to them whether they wish to change or not. All you can do is let them know how their behaviour makes you feel. If they care about you, they will choose to take account of that – provided it doesn't clash with any of their real wants.

The only time it is really appropriate to give advice is when the other person asks for it. If you do give advice, it should always be offered as a *suggestion*, respecting the other's freedom to accept it or not.

Finally, avoid being too analytical. The other person wants to know how you *feel* – not how clever you are. Feelings bring you to a deeper level of relating. They may be irrational, or put a blemish on your spotless self-image, but they reveal who you are on a deeper level. There is an innocence and spontaneity about feelings which brings you closer to a person's heart – something which no amount of intellectual discussion can achieve.

In the heat of the moment, however, it is easy to forget these things. We may say or do things which are hurtful and unloving. Relationships are sometimes messy and painful. Mistakes can be made. However, so long as both partners are sincere in their desire to learn and grow, there is no harm in making mistakes. After a fight or a falling out, it is good for each person to reflect on their behaviour, and consider whether they have done anything hurtful or unloving. If so, they should be willing to put their pride to one side, and acknowledge their mistake.

This is really the key to the growth and development of a relationship – acknowledging one's mistakes and saying sorry. Apologising, asking for and receiving forgiveness helps the hurt to melt, and the heart to reopen.

It is said that 'sorry' is the hardest word. In a sense, this is true. It is hard on the ego. Your pride will try to prevent you from saying the 's' word. You will rationalise your resistance by saying 'Oh, it will all blow over', or 'they'll get over it', or some such face saving statement. If you wish to choose pride over honesty, you will miss this opportunity to grow, and your relationship will not evolve to any depth.

Communication Skills

Sometimes we don't know if we have made a mistake or not. The other person may be hurt, but are we really to blame? Maybe it's just their problem.

It is true that not all hurts that our partner suffers are our responsibility. Sometimes they are hurt because of an unhealthy expectation or attachment they have which is not being fulfilled. We can empathise with them, but there is not much we can do about it. It is up to them to sort it out. However, there are times when our way of behaving or communicating causes them to react negatively. How do we distinguish between these two?

Psychologists have identified a number of 'communication roadblocks' – responses that have a high risk of generating a negative reaction in the other person. It is helpful to understand what these roadblocks are, so we can evaluate our behaviour in a more objective, rational way, and also learn effective communication skills.

These communication roadblocks tend to trigger a number of negative responses, including defensiveness, resistance, resentment, sense of inadequacy, withdrawal, despondency, and dependence. They decrease the chances of the other person opening up, sharing their feelings, discovering their own solution to the problem, and listening empathically.

Psychologist Robert Bolton, quoting Thomas Gordon in his book *People Skills*, lists a dozen communication roadblocks, and divides them into three categories, as follows:

1. JUDGING
   - Criticizing
   - Name-calling
   - Diagnosing
   - Praising inappropriately

2. SENDING SOLUTIONS
   - Ordering
   - Threatening
   - Moralising
   - Excessive/Inappropriate questioning
   - Advising

3. AVOIDING THE OTHER'S CONCERNS
   - Diverting
   - Logical Argument
   - Reassuring

The inappropriateness of most of these ways of relating in an intimate relationship is fairly self-evident, yet we are all apt to fall into one or more of these traps at different times. Having this list in mind helps us to evaluate our behaviour as we reflect in a cooler, more rational fashion after the heat of the battle.

How, then, should we communicate? If this is what doesn't work, then what does?

In communicating effectively, it is important to have both the right skills, and the right attitude.

Communication skills include the ability to listen empathically, and to express your wants and needs clearly. Listening empathically means that you really hear both the content and the feelings of what the other person is saying, and you can reflect that back to them. You do not try to fix them up, or correct what they say, or judge them, or advise them, or give an opinion, or in any way interfere with what they are saying. You simply listen and reflect back. At the most, you may ask a question to clarify what they are saying or encourage them to open a little more. Reflecting back lets them know you have heard and understood what they have said. E.g. you may say, 'You are angry because I am not spending enough time with you'. A simple statement that reflects to them that you have heard and understood both the feeling and content of what they are saying.

Empathic statements usually take the form of 'You feel….. because…….'

That is all you say. Remember, you are not trying to fix things up. Neither are you trying to justify yourself. *You are just listening*, and letting the other person know that you have heard and understood. This kind of empathic listening is an essential skill to good communication. It is not an easy skill to master. We are so used to giving opinions, interrupting, justifying, advising, praising, blaming etc., that we rarely practise this simple art of empathic listening.

When a person feels they are being listened to empathically, they will open up more. If there are no judgements, opinions, advice etc. coming back at them, something in them relaxes. They feel this person is interested in what I have to say, and furthermore their interest is non-threatening. I don't have to defend myself, or justify myself with this person. A trust develops. Communication flows more openly and deeply.

The other important aspect of effective communication is to express or assert your wants and needs. We have spoken about this earlier in this chapter.

The right attitude to communication is also of great importance. There are two aspects to this – sincerity and non-possessiveness. Communication is not just a matter of skill and technique. There needs be an underlying attitude of sincerity – i.e. a sincere wish to reach out, understand and share with the other person. And we must be non-possessive – i.e. we must be willing to respect the autonomy of the other. If someone is to feel safe enough to open up to us, they must genuinely feel that we have their best interests at heart. That we are not trying to subtly manipulate and control them for our own benefit. That we are there for them, that we will always respect and support their soul's purpose, even if it takes them away from us.

This is not an attitude we can fake. The other person will sense intuitively if we are there for them or not. If we find ourselves struggling with these issues, we need to take some time out to reflect on our possessiveness and our desire to control, and make a sincere effort to give up these attitudes. They will undermine our relationships more than any lack of skill or technique.

Power and Sex

When it comes to developing non-possessiveness, the issue we probably have most trouble with is the almost universally prevalent idea that if you are in a sexual relationship with someone – then they somehow *belong* to you. They are *yours*. Our language reflects this idea in many ways. We speak of wanting to *make you mine*. The other person is *my partner, my husband, etc.*

In the previous chapter we saw how sexual possessiveness is part of the animal side of our nature. It is an unconscious, instinctual urge. This urge is so powerful, and the effects of frustrating it are so damaging, that society has decided to sanction possessiveness as a legal right. Once two people are married, then in many ways their lives become intertwined – financially, sexually, legally, socially. The law and the society recognise that a married couple belongs exclusively to each other. What society is, in effect, saying is that it does not consider its members to be mature enough to handle a non-possessive relationship. It considers that, for most people, their sexual possessive instincts are so uncontrollable, that they will likely go berserk if they don't have a firm legal hold over their partner.

This social norm has become part of our conditioned way of thinking also. We think it is normal to feel possessive about our partner. When the sexual energy starts to move to the power chakra, this feeling of possessiveness starts to extend from the sexual to other areas of our partner's life. We think we have a right to advise them and tell them what to do. Sexual possessiveness mixed with the unconscious energy of the power chakra becomes a very volatile mix. People in the grip of this energy can become very irrational, controlling and violent.

We have looked at how to deal with sexual possessiveness in the last chapter. The challenge at this third chakra is to prevent our feeling of possessiveness from spreading from the sexual area into other areas. We do this by consciously opposing the social norms we are surrounded by, and listening to our intelligence instead.

Our intelligence will tell us that:
- We do not own anyone
- Our partner is an autonomous being – they do not belong to us.
- We have no right to dictate or decide what our partner should do
- To create the possibility of a loving connection with our partner, we need to approach them in a non-possessive way
- If we want our partner to respect our freedom, we need to do the same for them
- To love someone is to honour and support their soul's purpose

Power and Emotion

The power chakra, and hence the choices we make, are to a large extent controlled by our emotions. It is human nature to choose that which gives pleasure and joy, and to avoid that which gives pain and sorrow. Our emotions, our feelings, are the single most powerful factor in determining the shape and direction of our lives.

If we could be innocent and spontaneous with our feelings, this would not be a problem. In children we can see how these qualities lead to a state of trust and non-attachment, and to a lack of craving and desire for control. Listening to our real feelings spontaneously gives a right direction and sense of purpose to our lives.

Unfortunately, as adults, we often lose this ability to be innocent and spontaneous. Our feelings and emotions are no longer connected to and influenced by our real selves (our heart and soul). Instead, they become influenced by our ego and our conditioned self.

Generally speaking, our conditioned self operates out of fear, and our ego operates out of pride. As we become adults, the emotions of fear and pride dominate the choices we make more and more.

It is *fear* that causes us to choose security over adventure, and comfort over creativity. Fear blinds us to our true potential, and causes us to make choices that are safe and predictable. Fear leads to dullness and rigidity, and an excessive need to control the circumstances of our lives. Life itself is constantly changing, and the joy of being alive comes from flowing with the changing circumstances of life.

Egoic pride causes us to make choices that enhance our self-image. We chase after wealth and status, often to the detriment of our health and wellbeing. We choose a partner based on their appearance or social standing. How we appear to others becomes more important than being true to ourselves. When our self-image is threatened, we get angry or hurt or defensive. We fear any loss of status. We'll go to great lengths to avoid anything that might cause shame or humiliation. The whole of our emotional lives becomes caught up in how we are seen by others. These emotions then determine the choices we make.

I am not suggesting that we should abandon security and ego altogether. Everyone needs a certain sense of security and stability in their lives. And developing a healthy ego, and a pride in one's work and achievements, is a necessary part of our psychological development. What is important is that we keep these things in perspective. Security and ego are not everything in life. They are just one aspect, one small portion of our total needs. If we place too much emphasis on them, we will suffer. Our development will get stuck here at the power chakra, and we will never know the greater joy that opening the heart can bring.

It is fear and ego, and the excessive desire for control that they bring, which create the major blockages at the power chakra.

In order for our energy to flow freely from the third to the fourth chakra, we need to learn to give up wants and desires based on fear and ego. We need to understand our ego – which part of it is healthy, and which part is unhealthy. Generally speaking, the healthy part of our ego is that which is in harmony with our true self. The unhealthy ego is that which is concerned with our self-image.

When we are making choices based on our real needs, and on our soul's purpose, we will find that joy spontaneously enters our lives, and the power chakra no longer blocks the upward flow of energy.

Power and Love

Ask any psychotherapist or healer "What is the central issue your clients struggle with?", and they will say "Love".

Ask them "What is the one thing that will bring lasting happiness and wellbeing?", and they will say "Love".

Read accounts of people who have had NDE's (Near Death Experiences), and the one thing they all report is a recognition that the most important thing in life is "Love".

Whenever we examine the core of our lives, and ask ourselves what is the most important thing that will bring me happiness and fulfillment – the answer invariably is "Love". Often it takes some intensive inner self-exploration, or a life crisis, to make us aware of this fact. Far too often, we become pre-occupied with non-essentials – work, pleasure, career, ambitions, appearance, entertainment etc. and lose sight of our soul's need for love.

In order to find love, we have to make it a priority. We have to choose it. We have to say 'I want love', and make that want more important than any other. Then we start to use the energy of the power chakra in a positive way.

Unfortunately, love never seems to make it to the top of our list of priorities. Or we think that we don't have to search for love – it will somehow magically find us.

It is true that love will find you – if you are willing and ready to be found. There is a poem by the Sufi mystic, Rumi, which goes:

The wine of God's grace is infinite
The only limitation comes from your cup
Moonlight floods the whole sky from horizon to horizon
How much of it enters your room depends on your window

So the question becomes – is your cup free of cracks? Are your windows free of dust? In other words, are you receptive to God's version of love, or are you only looking for your own version?

Most of us will say we want love – but do we really know what that is? Would we recognise it, or know what to do with it, if it arrived? Are we really looking for the reality of what moves in the heart, or are we looking for our *idea* of love? What is our idea of love? To what extent are we caught up in the Hollywood version? The romanticised, sanitised, idealised, pop song version? How realistic is our idea of love?

When you really start to look for love, these questions take on a great importance. Many of us have had the experience of falling in love, thinking we have found 'the one', only to see the relationship fall apart at the first hurdle. Wanting love is one thing – knowing what to look for, and how to nurture it, is something else.

You can use the energy of the power chakra to help you to find love. In order to do this effectively there are two things you need to do:

1. You have to put "Love" at or near the top of your list of priorities. You have to say "I want love", and put your whole energy into doing whatever it takes to find it.

2. You have to develop a clear idea of what love really is,
    so that you can recognise it and be receptive to it when it
    'enters your window' and 'fills your cup'.

Once your energy of power is engaged with these two things, then
the arrival of love in your life is almost guaranteed. In this way, the
power chakra, rather than hindering your quest for love, will be a
great ally in helping you to find it.

The question of what love really is we will explore in the next
chapter.

Power and You

From the preceding discussion, we can see that the energy of the
power chakra can be a friend or an enemy, depending on how you
use it.

The power chakra is located between the sex chakra and the
heart chakra. It can act either as a barrier, preventing energy from
reaching to the heart, or as a bridge allowing its free passage. It
becomes a barrier when it is used unconsciously and destructively.
When it is blindly linked to the negative aspects of sexuality – possessiveness and jealousy – and used to control and dominate the
other. And when it is used to bolster and promote unhealthy aspects
of our ego.

It becomes a bridge when it is used consciously and construc-
tively. When we sincerely learn to communicate effectively with our
partner in a non-possessive way, and when we empower our longing
for love by making the quest for love a priority.

The power chakra is about making choices. Rarely in history
have people had the freedom of choice that we enjoy today. It is up
to you to use this freedom wisely. In spite of the lack of role models,
in spite of the poor choices that others seem to be making, you are
free in every moment to raise your sights, to make a pact with the
universe and an uncompromising commitment to yourself. You are
free to choose love.

Choice and Karma

There is a Zen saying 'He treads the sharp edge of the sword. He runs over the steep ridge of the iceberg'. This reminds us that our lives are always finely poised. The choices we make in each moment determine the quality of the next moment. Life is dynamic, and is always moving in either a positive or negative direction. There is a delicate balance in our lives, and each choice we make contributes something – for good or for bad. We cannot remain neutral, or static, or detached. Choosing wisely is a major factor in the art of living.

The theory of Karma reinforces this. Karma may be summed up by the statement that 'we reap what we sow'. Our thoughts, our choices, our actions create ripples that impact others, and then bounce back to impact us at some future time. The theory of Karma states that you are responsible for your present existence, and for what you will become. Your future depends on the choices you make now.

Chapter 6

===

Heart

As you start to practice the suggestions and processes described in the previous three chapters, more energy will be available to rise to, and awaken the heart. At this point you can hear love knocking on your door. Another world is opening up for you.

This is the moment when the question 'What is Love?' becomes relevant. Often our illusions about love will prevent us from recognising the real thing when it comes along. We may hear it knocking – and decide it is just the wind. Or we are afraid to grasp the handle and open the door.

We all have some resistance to opening our hearts. Love rarely enters our lives in a smooth, straightforward way. Our resistance comes from different places – both personal and cultural. There is, in our culture, an enormous amount of ignorance about the true nature of love. This ignorance causes us to try to bend love into all kinds of unnatural shapes. We want our relationships to fit with our ideas of how they should be. We are not willing to listen to our hearts and let love inform us of how it wants to be. No – we insist on having love our way.

Our ignorance of the nature of love is one of the main causes of the grief and heartache we suffer in relationships. Much of the pain we experience in relationships is avoidable. Our inherited cultural ignorance makes things far more difficult than they need to be.

In the first part of this chapter, we will explore the question of what love is. We will look at the common illusions that exist about love, and try to understand something of its true nature. This understanding will help you to get your relationships right. Love will never fit in with your ideas. Nobody can make water flow uphill. Things don't happen that way. There are natural laws that apply to the flow of love. Once you understand them, then love has a chance of becoming a reality in your life.

People often find that, just when love is ready to open up for them, they sabotage it in some way. A resistance to accepting love arises. When it comes to love, we human beings are complicated creatures. Love itself is simple, but we seem to be very creative at muddling things up. In the second part of this chapter, we will examine the seven ways in which we block the flow of love.

Finally, we will look at how we can create the right climate in which love can bloom. Creating the right climate is not just about choosing an exotic incense and some funky African music. There are certain attitudes and behaviours that encourage the heart to open. We will look at how to cultivate these.

Recognising Illusions about Love

When a rose bush starts to bloom, we know what to expect. We don't stand around waiting for little green men to pop out. However, when we enter a relationship, our expectations are often for little green men – singing, dancing, signing cheques and bearing gifts. Many of us have all sorts of illusions about love. Parents, friends, movies, novels all pander to our illusions, and lead us to expect something quite unrealistic.

The fantasies and illusions that people have about love have changed in recent years. We are familiar with what our parents and grandparents used to swoon over – knights in shining armour; riding off into the sunset hanging on to Clark Gable; the 'happily ever after' of domestic bliss. A few of these old fashioned fantasies still linger in some peoples minds, but most of us have moved on from there.

What we now imagine love to be is a more subtle and insidious illusion. The current daydream is a narcissistic one. People now imagine love to be a form of mutual ego stroking. Love has been defined as 'how good the other person can make you feel about yourself'. The problem is we confuse our self-image with our self. Hence we over-emphasise the image we project. In love we want to be admired. We seek to impress others with how we look, what we have achieved, and how successful and knowledgeable we are. The current myth that moves people now is the myth of Narcissus.

In this myth, the youth Narcissus sees his reflection in a pool of water. He becomes so captivated by his reflection that he loses all awareness of himself, till he eventually starves to death gazing at himself reflected in the pool.

This is what many lovers nowadays seek to do. They look for someone who will reflect their image back to them in such a way that they become enraptured with themselves. Men seek women to appreciate and praise them, and women do the same thing. Each person becomes a pool of water for the other, reflecting back an enhanced self-image to his or her partner.

If our chosen pool of water starts reflecting unpleasant things back to us, we become very disturbed. They may be telling us some truth about ourselves, but this is not what we want to hear. We are not really interested in the other person, but only in what they can reflect back to us about ourselves.

Eventually, like Narcissus, we lose awareness of ourselves, and become starved – of genuine companionship and of love.

Narcissism is the current illusion many people have about love. It can seem like love, because when we love we also have an admiration for our beloved. However, the narcissist is more concerned with what the other person thinks of them, than with how they feel towards their partner. Their feelings for their partner are almost entirely dependent on how much positive feedback their partner gives – and can evaporate as soon as the praise dries up.

Narcissism is insidious because it is so widespread and difficult to detect. Ask yourself if you depend heavily on your partner's praise? How do you react to any criticism from your partner? If your partner is in a bad mood, do you take it personally? Are you aware of feeling the need to praise your partner often? Are you afraid to offer any sort of criticism or complaint to them? How dependent are you on your partner's good opinion? Your responses to these questions will give you an indication of the extent to which you confuse narcissism with love.

The other illusion many people have about love is the 'happily ever after' one. We still believe that love should last forever – that there will be one person who we can be with in a loving relationship for the rest of our lives. This idea has probably caused more heartache down the ages than any other. When our 'happily ever after' dream turns sour, we find ourselves completely at a loss. We feel trapped. We don't have the skills to improve the situation, and we are unable to leave.

Anyone caught in this situation should recognise two things. Firstly, experiencing difficulties in a relationship is what you are there for. There is no 'happily ever after'. We enter relationships in order to face challenges and learn lessons. If you can accept this, then you create the possibility of re-opening the flow of love in your relationship. This can happen by you acquiring the skills necessary to meet the challenges of a relationship. We will look at how to acquire these skills later in this chapter.

Secondly, while it is true that the state of love itself can – and does – last forever, there is no universal law that says it should be with only one person. Love can continue in many forms, with many people. The idea that love should last with a particular person is a socially conditioned one – that does not always turn out to be the case in reality. This does not mean that it can never happen. Some people do maintain a loving relationship for many years. It does mean, however, that for other people this will not be the case.

These are the common illusions we have about love. What, then, is love? What is its true nature?

The Nature of Love

Love is an energy that arises spontaneously in the heart. There is nothing we have to do to make it happen. Love is our intrinsic nature. It is already the case. If we are not experiencing love right now – it's not because we are failing to create it. Not at all. The only

reason we don't experience love right now is because we are preventing it from arising. We are blocking its flow.

We are usually not aware of doing this. It happens unconsciously.

When we notice that love is not flowing in us, one of the biggest
mistakes we make is to try to make it happen. Real love is spontaneous. Trying to create it just produces a phoney kind of love, and our
efforts become one more barrier to the flow.

We can think of love as like water flowing in a stream. Our illusions about love are like dams across the stream, blocking its flow.
When we see the flow is dammed up, it doesn't help to jump into the
stream with a paddle and start trying to move the water along. What
we have to do is remove the dam.

We will look at how to remove obstacles to the flow of love in
the next section. For now, we want to get clear about what love is. We
need to understand that there is an infinite wellspring of love already
present in our hearts. We don't have to make love happen. It is
already there, waiting to be allowed to flow.

The second thing about the nature of love that we need to understand is that love only ever happens in the Now. Love is like every
other aspect of life in this regard. We only connect to life in the
present moment. Our breath is happening now. Our heartbeat is
happening now. Our hearts are not thinking about how they can
keep on beating for the next twenty five years. All of life is simply
here and now.

While life and love both happen in the Now, there is a difference
between them. Life's processes are anchored in the physical world,
whereas love is not. Life belongs to the physical body, whereas love
belongs to something beyond the physical.

Life belongs to the first three chakras, whereas love is the energy
of the fourth chakra.

It so happens that most of our day-to-day activities are caught
up with the energies of the first three chakras. These three chakras
involve our interaction with the physical world – the world of work,
money, family, social and political activity. All these activities take

place in the earthly realm of space and time. We move from home, to work, to the supermarket, to the gym etc. – all according to a certain time frame or schedule. So, in our daily lives, our awareness of time becomes very highly developed. We are always looking at our watches, not wanting to be late.

We could say that, of the seven chakras, the first three belong to the earth plane, and the last three belong to the sky or spiritual plane. The heart – the fourth chakra – exists in between these two, and is the link between earth and spirit.

So when our energy reaches to the heart we are, in an almost literal sense, taking a jump out of the earth plane. We are suddenly not as earth-bound as we were before. Our involvement with the ordinary, mundane world is reduced. Love gives us wings, and we have a sense of lightness, as though gravity has lost some of its hold on us. We may spend more time staring into space, sometimes in a kind of trance-like state. This is not idleness, but something akin to a meditative state.

This is why lovers like to spend time just lying in each others' arms. As energy reaches to the heart, we feel ourselves being released from the cares and pressures of the mundane world.

Another world opens up for us, where all is light and carefree.

When love happens to us, we enter another dimension. It is a dimension beyond space and time. When we are in love, time stops. For a few moments, or a few hours, when our beloved is there, we become like children again – oblivious of time. Like someone in deep meditation, we have a glimpse of the Eternal, the Timeless.

If we are unfamiliar with this state, we can misinterpret this experience. We take the sense of the Eternal to be the same as that which is everlasting. This is why lovers so often feel that their love will last forever. It is a natural mistake to make, but it leads to all kinds of trouble.

In reality, the Eternal and the everlasting are completely different states. The everlasting exists in time. It is just the future extending on and on from one year to the next. The Eternal exists out of time. Outside of time, there is no future. There is only the Now. And Now is not a part of time.

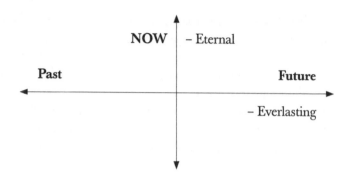

If the movement of time from past to future can be represented by a horizontal line, then the Now is a vertical line which penetrates time, and extends infinitely beyond it into another dimension. The Now has height and depth. It is where the spiritual intersects the physical. Each small movement of time ushers in a new Now. So the Now is always new, and the Now never ends. In this sense, the Now is Eternal and the Eternal is Now.

Love is connected to the Eternal. So love only ever happens in the present moment. It goes against the nature of love to think we can preserve it into the future.

It is not easy for our ordinary minds to grasp this, because we are so used to thinking in terms of time and space.

Another way of putting it is that the first three chakras belong to the physical world of space and time, and love belongs to the fourth dimension. When you start considering your love to be a part of time – e.g. you try to preserve your love into the future – you are trying to *pull it down* from the fourth dimension into the 3D world of space and time. This is against the nature of love. It is like trying to make a chair fit onto a flat sheet of paper. It won't work, and if you do succeed the chair will be destroyed.

Without realising it, this is what we are doing every time we try to preserve our love for the future. The nature of love is to be Now. To keep love alive, we need to enter and stay in the present moment. If we start dreaming and projecting into the future, we lose touch with the Now – and love will start disappearing as surely as night follows day. And with it goes all possibility of happiness. Traditional commitment and dreams of the future create more misery in this world than anything else, because they destroy the only possibility of happiness – the arising of love in the Now.

You don't need to struggle with this issue. As your understanding of the nature of love grows, you will automatically stop creating dreams and expectations for the future. As your heart opens with someone, resist the urge to make too many promises for the future. Even if you do make plans together, make them with the understanding that you can never be certain about what the future will hold. Remain flexible. If you both stay in the Now moment, your love will stay alive, and this will automatically bring with it a commitment to support each other. Let love in the Now be your commitment, and you will discover the rewards of remaining in the present. As you stay in the present moment, you will experience that love remains alive for you. It will no longer just be words and empty gestures – efforts to fulfil past promises. It will remain new and fresh and spontaneous – and will continue to do so as long as it is meant to.

If your relationship does come to an end, there will be very little pain. You may feel some sadness – it will be a poignant moment – but you will recognise that the time has come to move on, and you will find that letting go is not difficult. You will be grateful to the other person for all that you have shared. And your heart will remain open and available for more love to come your way.

However, the more both of you stay in the present moment, in a non-possessive way, the greater is the chance that your relationship will grow and develop. You will discover an ever deepening delight in each other's company. You are likely to find that you spontaneously continue to seek each other out, and prefer each other's company.

These are the two major misunderstandings we have about the nature of love. We think we have to make it happen, and that it will last forever with one person.

When we understand that the nature of love is to be spontaneously abundant in the present moment, we can start to look at how we prevent that abundance from happening. How do we block its flow?

Removing Obstacles

There are a number of ways in which we prevent the flow of love from happening. If love is not happening in your life, rather than trying to figure out how to make it happen, ask yourself 'How do I block it?' The barriers that we place in the way of love are generally put there unconsciously. Other people may see what we are doing, but we are usually blind to it. The first step to removing obstacles is to *recognise that they are there*. Once we have seen them, then removing them becomes easy. It is just a matter of giving up old habits.

In this section we will examine some of the main roadblocks to love that people have. As you read through them, you may recognise that some of them reflect your own attitudes and behaviour. Rather than being dismayed at this, be grateful that you have learned something about yourself. This knowledge will help you to remove your own obstacles to love.

There are seven common ways in which we block the flow of love. These include :

1. Trying
2. Fear of pain
3. Projecting into the future
4. Demands and expectations
5. Attachment
6. Judgements
7. Control and manipulation

Let's look at each of these in turn.

1. Trying

Ordinarily, if we want something, we set out to try to make it happen. If we want to own a house, we have to work hard to earn the money. If we want to pass an exam, we have to study for many hours. In our minds we come to associate achieving goals with trying hard and making efforts.

When it comes to creating love, we automatically do the same thing. We start making all sorts of efforts – we cook special dinners, wear smart clothes, think of nice things to say, try to be supportive and so on. However, when we do these things, we find that we just get exhausted. Not only that, but our efforts are often unappreciated. We may think that more effort is required, and start wearing crystals, making positive affirmations, practicing forgiveness etc., – and still the amount of love we generate seems to be very meagre. We end up thinking that we must be surrounded by the world's most insensitive people.

The first thing to be understood in the quest for love is that we can't make it happen. You cannot create love through your own efforts. In fact, your efforts are a barrier to love. They block it. You have to see that your efforts come from a misunderstanding of the nature of love. Love is not a thing, like a house or a university degree. Love is an energy that arises spontaneously in the heart – when you get out of the way and stop interfering. Trying to create it doesn't work. This kind of effort is not helpful. As you start to recognise this, these efforts will drop of their own accord.

You also need to understand that you can't make someone else love you, neither can you expect or demand this from them. In fact, your efforts to appear loving are likely to put them off. To try to make someone love you is to be subtly manipulative. You are trying to influence their feelings towards you for your own benefit. They will sense this. Even if they play along with you, and everything seems lovey-dovey, the 'love' that you share will only be a superficial thing. You will miss the depth and reality of love.

This is not to say that you won't make efforts to share love, but your motivation will be different. Your efforts will not come from a desire to create something that isn't already there. They will be spontaneous, and will arise from a heart-felt wish to share in that moment.

I can remember when I first discovered this obstacle in myself. Even though I'd been in a relationship for some time, and things appeared to be going well between us, I kept feeling a sense of dissatisfaction. I couldn't understand where this feeling was coming from. I started to pay a little more attention to what was happening between us. I noticed that I would say things that I didn't really mean. I would say 'I love you' to my partner, even when I wasn't feel-ing anything very much at all. I was not speaking the truth in that moment. I was trying to make her feel good about being with me.

At other times, when she was hurt or disappointed, I would soothe her with pretty words, or else use my sharp tongue to justify myself and make her feel wrong. Then I would buy her gifts, or write a poem, just to make her feel better. I was creating feelings and expec-tations in her because I wanted her to see me as a loving person. I was being subtly manipulative, rather than truthful and honest.

As a result, I created a sense of togetherness and attachment in her that was not based on truth. And when she needed something from me, I resented it. My 'trying' had created a web in which I now felt trapped.

Seeing this was a humbling recognition. When I saw how I'd misled her by being manipulative and dishonest, I felt a real sense of shame. I took some time out from the relationship to give myself a chance to regain some clarity.

Reflecting on my past behaviour, I saw that I'd been trying too much to make a loving connection happen. I was good at creating what seemed to be a loving relationship, but a lot of it was a facade. I made a promise to myself to give up the games. No more pushing the buttons, cranking the levers, manipulating the situation to my advantage. No more *trying* to create love, either within myself or within a relationship anymore. From now on I would just be honest. I would begin by being true to myself, and bring that truth into my relationships.

I'd been unwilling to be honest, because I didn't feel OK with certain parts of myself. I didn't think my partner would find them acceptable or loveable. I decided that I would start with accepting and loving the truth of myself, as I am. And in relationship, I would give up the trying. If there was going to be any love in my life, it would have to come as a result of being honest – or not at all. If love could not abide the truth, then it was not worth having. I remem-bered the words of my spiritual teacher – 'Love is a by-product of truth' he'd said.

It was a great relief to give up the trying and the games. And my teacher has proved to be right. My relationships since then have taken on a totally different quality – something far more real, and more loving.

To find a love that is real, you need to give up your ego's efforts to make it happen. Don't try to be loving. Just be true to yourself. Be honest. *The truth of yourself is love*, and honesty with yourself and others will reveal this.

You can start this process by adopting a simple mantra. Ask yourself "What is in my heart right now?" Then just feel and listen. Give up all efforts to influence your feelings. Don't try to feel love or anything in particular. Just allow your heart to reveal itself to you. Accept whatever is there, without judgement, or wishing it was different.

You may discover a tightness, or numbness, or even pain. Accept these feelings without trying to change them. Let your heart have its own life. There is a poetry to heartache, and a depth to sadness that gives an extra colour and dimension to our lives. Learn to accept all the seasons of your heart, and it will reveal more and more of its mystery and wonder to you.

Let this question "What is in my heart right now?" become a part of you. Let it become a koan – something you carry with you and investigate as often as possible during each day. Let the spirit of this question infuse your heart and mind.

For many people this will require a leap of faith. You will feel like you are not in control any more. And in a sense, this is true. Opening the heart requires a letting go, and a trust in the innate goodness of the energies of the heart. You may wonder – what if I discover too much pain, or that I don't love my partner anymore?

The quest for love is only for the courageous. If you are courageous, you will want to know if you still love your partner or not. Your quest for love will prefer the truth. You will not want to pretend for the sake of comfort and convenience.

In the quest for love, our commitment changes. We become committed not to a single person, but to the truth of love. We may share our quest with another, but each will be committed to learning and sharing the truth. As we learn to discover and accept our own truth, it will be easier to accept the truth of the other person.

The love we create through our own efforts turns out to be an artificial sort of love. To know the real fragrance of the rose flower, we need to be willing to surrender to what is in our hearts.

2. Fear of pain

One of the main reasons people remain closed at the heart is that love brings with it the possibility of pain. Heartache is perhaps the most devastating form of pain we can experience, and the fear of it causes many people to remain guarded at the heart. This self-protection becomes a barrier that blocks the flow of love. If we have been hurt in the past, we can start to play it safe, keeping the deeper and more vulnerable parts of ourselves shut out from a relationship.

There are two things we need to understand about the relationship between love and pain.

Firstly, it is not love itself that causes pain. We experience pain because of our attitudes and beliefs about love. These include the idea that love will last forever, and the dreams and expectations we create from this idea. We have talked about this issue in the previous section on the nature of love. We will discuss it in further detail in the next section. It is quite possible to enter and leave a relationship with little or no pain, provided we do so with the right attitude.

Secondly if pain does arise, we need to deal with it in an effective way. Let's look at how this can be done.

Dealing with Pain

When a relationship breaks down, it is mostly experienced as painful. It can be a pain that is sudden and devastating, or slow and insidious. In either case, it needs to be dealt with.

People have different ways of dealing with pain. Often the pain is experienced as being too much to bear, and the person tries to avoid it. They will distract themselves with work, or alcohol, or shopping trips or complaining to their friends. Others will try to talk themselves out of feeling the pain. They'll spend hours in rationalising, reviewing, blaming, mental juggling and feeling sorry for themselves.

These efforts are mostly ineffective, and usually just achieve a hardening of the heart into resentment and bitterness, and a closing down into self-protection.

It is difficult to accept the pain that accompanies the break-up of a relationship. Yet if we want to remain openhearted and available to love, then this is exactly what we must do. How do we go about this?

There is a saying that 'Pain is unavoidable, but suffering is optional'. This means that a pure and simple heart-ache will always accompany a romantic dream that is broken, but the mental anguish, brooding, blaming and other contortions we go through in order to avoid this pain are 'optional' – in the sense that if you are intelligent you wont indulge in them.

When dealing with a relationship break-up, you firstly need to recognise that *you cannot think your way out of the pain.* The pain is unavoidable, and no amount of rationalising, or mental control will change that. All you will achieve is to repress the pain – which generally leads to an excessive and compulsive brooding over past events. You need to stop thinking and just allow yourself to feel the pain. Feel it as a sadness, or as a heart-ache – a burning in the chest. The pain needs to be released from the heart.

To do this, lie down somewhere when you won't be disturbed, and bring your attention inside the body. It is here, in the body, where your feelings are. Relax, and breathe into the belly and the chest, and feel what is happening there. Allow the feelings to come up, and be released. As you do this, recognise that your pain is perhaps about a number of things – rejection, abandonment, betrayal – and allow the pain and hurt associated with each of these things to simply run its course. To help this process, use visual images. Visualise the person you are separating from, and allow your feelings to arise as you see the person in your mind's eye. Keep your breathing relaxed and open. See the situation, and let the images you have trigger your feelings. Finally, recognise that the greatest pain comes from the fact that the dreams and expectations you had for that relationship have been broken. Allow yourself to grieve the loss of your dream, and feel the hurt of the separation.

I have taken many people through this process, and they all report the same sense of surprise – that when the pain is faced it turns out to be bearable! It is not half as bad as they had been imagining. By allowing the pain to run its course in this way, you will soon find that you are becoming free of it. In my experience, by not indulging the mental suffering, but simply dealing with the pain effectively, it is possible to get over a relationship break-up in a matter of days or weeks, rather than months or years.

This process needs to be gone through whether you are the one initiating the break-up or not. Both partners will have had their dreams and attachments within the relationship, and even if you initiate the break-up, some loss and pain will still need to be released.

The same applies to past break-ups for which the grieving and releasing of pain has not been allowed to run its course. If you still think about a past relationship a lot, going over what went wrong in your mind, it is likely that the pain has not been fully released.

(There is also a possibility that you are carrying pain from past childhood hurts and neglects. These can impact a relationship in all sorts of ways. It is often necessary to free yourself of these before you can enter an adult relationship in an emotionally clear way. It is beyond the scope of this book to discuss how this can be done. This issue is discussed in depth in the books of John Bradshaw and others.)

As you go through the process of feeling and releasing pain, you will eventually become free of it. At a certain point, you will find that the feeling has run its course, and there is no more pain. Then you can productively start to review and understand the causes of the pain. How, by projecting into the future and creating dreams and attachments, you have contributed to the pain you have just been suffering. Forgive yourself, and your partner, for whatever role each of you played in the break-up. And feel grateful to your partner for the love you have shared, and the lessons you have learned.

This will free you up to move on in life without any of the emotional baggage and bitterness so many people accumulate. Your heart will once more be open and free to love again.

3. Projecting into the future

If pain arises, the intelligent thing to do is to look into the attitudes and beliefs that have created it – and drop them. Then pain serves a useful purpose. It is not there to put us off love, or to make us guarded and defensive. It is there to awaken us to the foolishness of some of our attitudes and beliefs about love.

What are the attitudes and beliefs that lead to pain?

We get hurt because of our dreams and expectations and attachments to love. When we fall in love with someone, we imagine it will last forever. We start dreaming of the future, and lose touch with the here and now. As we have seen, the nature of love is such that it only ever arises in the here and now. Love is a spontaneous arising of energy in the heart. We cannot predict what this energy will do in the future. It may continue to arise with someone, or it may not. It may fluctuate. Yet when it arises, it is such an overwhelming experience, that we simply can't imagine how it could ever disappear. We are convinced that it will last forever.

As a result, we start creating dreams and expectations for the future. We get attached to the feeling of love, and to the person who has helped to awaken it in us. Our family and friends are likely to encourage us in forming this attachment. The whole society believes in the permanence of love, and the validity of commitment, and in making dreams for the future. So we feel completely at ease in allowing our imagination free rein.

We are not content to be loved *now*. Rather than simply enjoying the beauty of love in this present moment, we become more concerned with how to preserve this feeling into the future. As if love in this universe is so limited, that this person represents our one and only chance of sharing love in this lifetime. It is our fear of losing love, and our ignorance of the nature of love that causes us to do this. Yet this fear and ignorance, and the dreams and attachments they create, are so common and widespread, we rarely pause to consider if what we are doing makes sense.

Love is only experienced in the now. By losing touch with the here and now, we lose touch with love also. Paradoxically, in trying so hard to preserve our love for the future, we destroy the very thing we are trying to preserve. As far as love is concerned, our efforts and energies should be directed to sharing in the present moment. When we start projecting into the future, we lose touch with the present and we accelerate the loss of the relationship. Our dreams and expectations for the future, and the promises and commitments we make, are almost impossible to actually fulfil. When someone starts slipping up on their promises, we get into blaming and demanding. Arguments develop. We start thinking we are entitled to the love and commitment that was promised, and feel justified in making all sorts of demands.

Then, if a separation does occur, rather than being grateful for the love you have shared, you will be devastated – because your dreams and hopes have been shattered. Love does not cause pain. Pain comes from broken dreams and expectations. Dreams that you create out of your own fear and ignorance. The pain is not there to put you off love for the rest of your life, but to make you more aware of the inappropriateness of projecting into the future.

Next time you start a relationship, or if you are currently in a relationship, catch yourself each time you start dreaming about the future. Watch your thoughts, and don't let them wander aimlessly. Whenever you catch yourself, make an effort to bring yourself back to the here and now. Come back to your mantra "What is in my heart right now?" In this way, a loving relationship becomes like a meditation. The aim of meditation and the aim of love are the same – to be present in the here and now. Each time you do this, you create the possibility of your heart opening further. And you avoid the possibility of pain should your relationship happen to end. If there are no dreams to be broken, then if a relationship does finish, there will be little or no pain. Instead you will be grateful to your partner for all you have shared.

Projecting into the future is one of the main ways in which we block the flow of love. It takes us away from the only place where love is found – the Now moment. As we leave the Now, we are turning our backs on love. In so doing, we virtually guarantee one more heartache for ourselves.

4. Demands and expectations

Expectations are inner, silent demands. When expressed, they become outward, projected demands. When we have a preconceived idea of how a relationship should be, it creates an expectation in us. If our idea is based on an illusion, our expectations are unrealistic. When our expectations are not met, disappointment and frustration will follow.

We have talked about the common illusions people have about relationships – narcissism, 'happily ever after', dreams of the future. In addition to these, there are our own individual wishes and expectations around things such as tidiness, eating habits, social behaviour and so on. In these matters there needs to be some flexibility, and give and take.

Expectations become a barrier to the flow of love when they turn into demands. Demands are demeaning to the other person. They are disrespectful of their freedom. At the most, we can express our wishes in the form of a request, or a suggestion. We then leave it up to the other person whether they wish to comply or not.

If you are a demanding type of person, or if you carry unspoken expectations of what you want on the level of the heart, the first thing is to become aware of these things. Notice what effect your demands and expectations have on both yourself, and your partner. Feel your 'righteous indignation', and observe what the attitudes are that create it. Recognise that these attitudes may be coming from a sense of possessiveness or judgement. Or, there may be other feelings you have that contribute to your being demanding – a sense of dependency on your partner, or a sense of insecurity about yourself.

If you notice these things, rather than making your partner responsible for your wellbeing, accept responsibility for it yourself. Respect your partner's freedom to give and share with you as they wish, and do what you can to enhance your own wellbeing. If it is a deep-seated problem, go and seek some counselling. Otherwise, take time out for yourself, and reclaim your own independence. Explore ways outside of the relationship to find your own joy in life. As you free up your partner from a pattern of demands and expectations, it gives them the opportunity to spontaneously re-discover their love for you.

5. Attachment

Attachment is a kind of emotional dependency on another person. Attachment means that this person has met my needs for love and emotional closeness in the past, and I want them to continue doing that in the future. There is nothing wrong with wishing to continue to have intimacy with someone, so long as we don't wrap our emotional tentacles around that person. Attachment is an emotional clinging, which may cause the other person to feel stifled. Love can only grow in a climate of respect for the other's freedom. If we become too attached, our emotions will not allow the other person to be free, and in this way we may slowly strangle the love that is there.

If attachment is strong, it often comes from unresolved childhood issues, and you may need some therapy to overcome it. Another source of attachment is not having a sense of one's spiritual place in the universe – so one uses a relationship as a refuge from the world.

It is quite possible that having an attachment with someone is exactly what we need at this point in our lives. Each person is different, and we are all growing and evolving in our own way, and at our own pace. It takes a considerable amount of growth to reach a point where we can be emotionally non-attached, and yet still open hearted.

In the quest for love, however, it is something to be kept in mind – that attachment is a condition that will not allow the full flowering of the energies of the heart.

As we become more committed to discovering the truth of ourselves, we can use our attachments to others as a means of spiritual awakening. I can only be attached to someone if I have certain spiritual blind spots. If I am spiritually awake, I will recognise that there is no separate 'me' that is dependant on 'you' for love. I will see that each of us is connected to the source of love at all times, and that I don't need you to experience the fact that I am already 'in love'. At the very most, you give me the opportunity to share and express the love that I am.

If I notice that there is attachment in me, I can use this recognition to free myself of the conditioned thinking which creates it – the belief that 'I' exist as an independent entity; the belief that this 'I' is separate from others, and from existence. Buddhist teaching emphasises the importance of recognising the emptiness of all phenomena, including myself, as part of spiritual awakening. In this way, my relationships can become a vital part of my spiritual practice.

6. Judgements

There is a direct relationship between how little we judge, and our capacity for open-heartedness. I am not talking about legal judgements, or refereeing decisions, but judgements about ourselves and others. The more we judge, the more we feel bad about ourselves, and the more we shut the other person out.

It is one thing to be aware of something, it is quite something else to make a judgement about it. To take an example, let's say my belly is protruding. It is difficult not to be aware of this fact. Every time I look in the mirror, there it is staring back at me. Even if I don't happen to notice it, other people are sure to point it out to me. When I see my protruding belly, I can simply note its existence without comment or thought. Or I can make a judgement about it – "that's bad, that's unattractive, that shouldn't be there..." As I do this, my self-love diminishes.

Sometimes we try to counter our negative judgements with positive ones. "Hey, that belly isn't so bad. It looks rather dignified. It's a symbol of great prosperity..." This is what NLP practitioners call 'reframing'. It gives us a somewhat better feeling about ourselves, but it is still a judgment. It is best not to indulge in any judgement – either negative or positive. Judgement implies that we are measuring ourselves and others against some sort of standard. If we measure up we are 'good'. If we don't, we are 'bad' – and we 'should' do something about it. The three favourite words of the judgemental mind are 'good', 'bad' and 'should'.

The fundamental flaw with being judgemental is that it lacks acceptance of ourselves (and others) for where we are right now. Judgement is the main characteristic of the perfectionist and the idealist. And none of us are perfect. If perfection was the aim, we would all be entitled to spend half our lives sitting around beating ourselves up.

This doesn't mean we blindly accept everything about ourselves and others. We can maintain a discerning sense of discrimination and an evaluating awareness. However, we can do this without judgement. We just take note of our perceptions of ourselves and others without either condemning or excessively praising. We simply note that 'it is so'. This is what the Buddha refers to as seeing the 'suchness' of things.

There is a difference between making a judgement and an assessment. In judging something or someone, we call them either 'good' or 'bad', and we have an emotional reaction of acceptance or rejection towards them. In making an assessment there is no emotional reaction of this kind. We simply assess someone or something according to how they are, or how they serve my purpose in that moment. For example, if I need a car to get around in, I'll choose a car that suits my purpose. If the car is faulty, I will assess its faults and simply choose not to buy it. Similarly, if my purpose is to establish a loving relationship, I will choose someone suitable to that purpose. If I meet an uncaring, uncommunicative person who drinks excessively, I may decide that they do not serve my purpose in this moment, and choose not to pursue a relationship with them. This doesn't mean I am judging them. I am simply assessing them. The difference lies in how I feel towards them. In assessing them, I may still feel an empathy and compassion for them. In judging them, I invariably feel a sense of aversion and rejection towards them.

In an intimate relationship, and with ourselves, we do the same thing. We recognise our partner's positive qualities, and also their shortcomings. We don't call one 'good' and the other 'bad', and start trying to fix them. They will either get defensive, or feel inadequate. Either way, we have only managed to push them further away from us. If we accept their shortcomings without criticism or judgement, the whole gestalt changes. If we say to them, for example "Look, I know you have a fear around money/assertiveness/intimacy. It's OK. Let's not make it a problem. I can understand where you are at...' You can feel what kind of effect a statement like that might have on you. Something inside you relaxes. You feel accepted, supported, for where you are. You feel warmer towards your partner. And the problem starts to dissolve. When you accept someone *as they are*, without judgement, *their resistance to change starts to melt.*

The motivation for change has to come from within each person. If you are judging them and wanting them to change, you are simply creating a resistance in them. Acceptance creates the possibility of transformation of stuck issues. Judgement creates resistance, and makes them more stuck. Acceptance is what inspires the Jack Nicholson character in the movie 'As Good As It Gets' to say – 'you make me want to be a better man'.

7. Control and Manipulation

Love is not an energy that we can control and manipulate. It arises in a climate that is innocent, spontaneous, honest and non-possessive. Our efforts at control can happen in two ways – we can try to sabotage love that is arising, or we can try to make something happen that isn't there.

When love arises, a kind of surrender to it is required from us. This means that we need to put our ego aside, and relate from the heart in a spontaneous, innocent fashion. For those who are overly identified with their ego, this will be a challenging step to take. The ego perceives love as a threat to itself, and if it is not kept in check, will flip into all kinds of avoiding and sabotaging behaviours. Initially, love and ego are incompatible. We either relate from one or the other. If love is seen as a threat, we need to do some work on understanding and dis-identifying with the ego. Then we can become comfortable with accepting love, and sharing from the heart.

The effort to make love happen is also ego driven. This is the next stage of ego development, and occurs when the ego shifts gears from wanting to avoid love, to wanting to claim the credit for being

a great lover. Rather than waiting and allowing love to arise spontaneously, we start trying to prove how loving we are. We have spoken
about the futility of these efforts earlier in this chapter. In the next
chapter, we will see that the essence of love is spontaneity. There is
nothing we can do to make it happen. We also need to recognise
that there is nothing we can do about the way someone else feels
about us. They either love us or they don't. They either receive our
love, or they don't. They either open up to us, or they don't. Direct
or subtle efforts to manipulate how they feel are mostly counter-
productive.

When we recognise this, we will often experience a feeling of
helplessness. This is one of the most difficult feelings for many people to accept. Yet this feeling reflects a deep truth about our relationships with others. At bottom, there is nothing we can do for another
person, if they are not willing to be receptive. So we need to get comfortable with this feeling of helplessness, because it is part and parcel
of opening to love. With the energies of the heart, our ability to control is greatly limited. We may see things we don't like to see. We
may see that the other person really isn't interested in a loving relationship, or in being openhearted with us. It may be painful to recognise and accept this. Yet if this is the reality, the intelligent response
is to accept it, and if necessary feel the pain. There is no point in
wearing ourselves out with someone who is unresponsive. It is best
just to let them go and move on.

Even if it is painful, it will free us up to connect with someone
more responsive. The universe is abundant, and will always give us
what we need, if we remain available to it. And sometimes just the
act of letting go with someone takes a certain pressure off that person. This may free them up to re-discover their love for you.

People often react to efforts at helping or saving them. Our
efforts can create a resistance in them. When we let go, that resistance often melts – and the person finds it easier to reach out.

This is a lesson I had to learn as a counsellor and therapist. In
the beginning I would sometimes allow my desire to succeed with
someone intrude into the relationship between us. I noticed that
with a certain type of person, this desire on my part used to get their

back up – and undermine the trust between us. Since then I have learned to offer help or suggestions without any desire that these things should be accepted. I always allow the other person to choose whether they want to change or not.

These are the seven major obstacles whose presence will prevent the heart from opening spontaneously. It is worth repeating that we cannot create love ourselves. Our efforts should be directed to removing the obstacles that prevent love. These are like the pests that attack the rose flower and destroy it. If we can protect the flower from pests, it has a better chance of blossoming spontaneously.

Creating the Right Climate

In addition to protection from pests, a rosebush needs the right climate to blossom. We can help love to flourish by adjusting our attitudes and behaviours in certain ways. For example, love grows best when there is mutual trust. Trust creates an atmosphere in which the heart feels at ease. In this last section, we will look at ways in which you can create a climate that is conducive to the heart opening. These include:

1. Be here & now
2. Be non-possessive
3. Cultivate trust
4. Be honest & vulnerable
5. Practice the three A's
6. Practice forgiveness
7. Be grateful

1. Be Here and Now

We have seen that love only happens in the Now. To cultivate love, we need to bring ourselves into the present moment. One way to do this is to stop thinking and just look.

Research has shown that when we are thinking, our eyes wander. They move to the left or the right. This is an indication that we are not *present* with what is in front of us. We are wandering off. A similar thing happens in sleep. When we are dreaming, a phenomenon known as REM (Rapid Eye Movement) occurs, indicating a lot of brain activity. So an easy and effective way to bring yourself into the present moment is to keep your eyes steady. Look attentively. Make eye contact. Bring a sense of presence into your eyes. This will help your thoughts to slow down. Try it right now, as you read these words. There is a consciousness in each of us, which is always in a state of presence. It becomes obscured by too much mental activity, in the same way that the sky becomes obscured by clouds.

As your thinking reduces, gaps start appearing between the clouds. Your racing mind slows down and patches of blue sky appear. As you continue to let all thoughts, desires and plans disappear from your mind, the blue sky of conscious PRESENCE emerges within you. You ARE, but there is no thought.

When you are with your beloved, switch into this state of PRESENCE as much as possible. Let your eyes remain focused and steady. Don't talk too much about extraneous things. Keep the attention, and the conversation, anchored in the present.

Another simple way of staying present is to stop thinking and start feeling. Thinking is usually about something other than what is here and now. We are moving into the past, or the future, or to some other location. Feeling happens in the body, which is always Here. And feelings only ever arise in the present moment. They are always Now.

Feeling is the natural way in which the energies of the heart are expressed. The mind still plays a role in this, but it is a secondary one. The mind, or rather the awareness, perceives the feeling and finds a way of communicating it – verbally or non-verbally.

This is not to suggest that thinking should be abandoned altogether. Thinking and planning are helpful in the practical world.

However, if you wish to connect with something more than just the material plane, you need to learn how to switch your thinking on and off. To connect with the energies of the heart, we need to be able to travel between the two worlds – the world of time, and the world of the Timeless.

Switching from thinking to feeling helps to traverse these two worlds. We make a conscious decision to withdraw our energy from the activity of the brain, and bring ourselves into the body. Some physical exercise can assist in this transition. Meditation is also helpful in stilling the mind. As the mind slows down, pay attention to the feelings and sensations in the body. Don't analyse them, but simply experience them and be aware of them. Especially, pay attention to the feelings in the chest, around the heart area. Use your mantra "What is in my heart right now?" Learn to recognise and identify the different sensations, feelings and emotions that come and go.

Your feelings reveal the deeper layers of your self – your needs, your longings, your likes and dislikes, your fears, your joys, your aspirations. Sharing your feelings will create a greater intimacy with your partner. It opens up a more vulnerable part of yourself, and it is through vulnerability that our hearts are revealed to each other.

As we become familiar with both of these worlds, it becomes easier to pass back and forth between them. We develop a greater sense of detachment from the physical world, which brings a feeling of peace and tranquility. Many of the qualities that meditators spend years developing can be discovered simply through opening the heart.

2. Be non-possessive

The essential quality of an open heart is non-possessiveness. A non-possessive attitude respects the freedom of the other person. We recognise that they are here on this planet to fulfil their soul's purpose. And we have no right to control or influence how they go about doing this. One part of their soul's purpose may be to share a loving relationship with us – but we leave it up to them to decide how they wish to fulfil this.

At the same time, we claim for ourselves the same right not to be controlled or possessed by anybody. Just as we respect the other's freedom, we ask that they respect ours.

A non-possessive attitude on both sides is an essential starting point for a loving relationship. If one of the partners is unable or unwilling to cultivate this attitude, then as far as the heart is concerned, the relationship is unlikely to go very far.

Non-possessiveness allows the other person just to be themselves. They feel that they can relax in our presence. In this relaxed state, both people can discover deeper layers of themselves – creativity, stillness, insights and so on. A sharing can happen based on mutual positive regard and trust.

I once asked a friend of mine, who had been in a long-term relationship, what her secret was for staying together for so long. She replied, half-jokingly 'Having a joint mortgage'.

From a practical point of view, it is easier to cultivate an attitude of non-possessiveness if both partners are financially independent. Unless both are evolved to the point where they have little or no attachment to money, any sort of financial enmeshment is likely to muddy the waters. A non-possessive attitude means, essentially, that we are willing to let go of the relationship if that's what our higher self or higher purpose requires for us. Not being financially enmeshed will make this attitude easier to maintain for most people.

What about sexual possessiveness? This really depends on how open-hearted you want to be. Generally speaking, the more we can be non-possessive in all areas of the other person's life, the greater is the possibility for open-hearted sharing. Being sexually non-possessive means being willing to sacrifice short term pleasure and intimacy for the sake of honouring and respecting the other's freedom. It requires a strong sense of trust and acceptance – qualities which we will discuss later in this chapter.

At the same time, we don't want to compromise our own genuine needs – and if our need at this time is for monogamy in a relationship, we ought to honour that need in ourselves, and ask our partner to do the same.

The main problem most couples have with sexual liaisons outside of the relationship is that these are usually conducted in secret – without the knowledge or consent of the other person. This is a violation of trust and a disregard of the needs and feelings of one's partner. My suggestion for anyone contemplating a fling is to let your partner know what is going on – and let them decide if they can accept you having a fling or not. This will give them plenty to think about in terms of where they stand regarding possessiveness, honouring your freedom, and so on.

Apart from money and sex, our strongest attachment is to love itself. Love is something that is relatively rare in the many encounters we have with other people – especially love of an intimate nature. So when we find it, our tendency is to cling to it. An attachment develops, and the relationship inevitably turns sour. This is why love in most relationships doesn't last much past the honeymoon. In the beginning we are non-possessive and non-attached – naturally so, because we have only just met the person. By chance, some love has passed between us. We feel a heart connection opening up. We are thrilled. We find ourselves singing love songs in the shower – songs like the old chestnut 'love and marriage go together like a horse and carriage'. Then within a few days or weeks – Kazzoom!! – the tentacles go out, and the clinging starts. All of a sudden, we feel less wonderful. We feel stifled, suffocated. And the next thing we know is, the song in the shower has become 'Bye, Bye, Love".

To avoid the inevitable descent into the loveless mediocrity that most relationships slide into, from the very start practice non-possessiveness. Rather than singing about 'Love and Marriage', sing about 'Love and Non-possessiveness' instead. At the start, in the middle, and at the end – practice non-possessiveness. If you can carry this mantra in your heart, then even if you do get married, your love will continue to deepen and grow every day.

To strengthen the attitude of non-possessiveness, there is one other quality we need to develop – the quality of trust.

3. Trust

Trust operates on two levels – the human and the divine. On the human level, we may learn over time to trust our partner, within human limits. We may recognise that they have honesty, integrity and goodwill. And that their word can be relied on. Yet, in the human realm, our trust is never absolutely confident. People can let us down at times, either intentionally or unintentionally. No matter how committed someone may be to a relationship, there are always factors that impact on our lives which are beyond our control. None of us can look into our own souls and read the whole script. Destiny or karma may take us in directions we hadn't anticipated. An irresistible job offer, a meeting with a soul mate or spiritual teacher, a death in the family, a sudden loss of health – events like this will have a significant impact on the dynamics of a relationship. Our partner may suddenly want to go and support an aging parent, or go on a six-month journey of self discovery.

Trust in the divine means that, even if we don't see all of the bigger picture, we trust that by letting go, being non-possessive, allowing our partner freedom, claiming freedom for ourselves – the universe will be taking care of both of us. It is only with this kind of trust that an attitude of non-possessiveness can grow and develop.

Trust in the universe is not just a mental thing. On a deeper level, it is a state of the heart. It is the same trust a small child has in a benevolent parent leading it by the hand across a busy street.

If this trust is not already a part of your nature, it can be cultivated. We have discussed how to cultivate trust in the third chapter.

4. Honesty and Vulnerability

The more you can open up to someone, the greater the intimacy that can develop. Honesty and vulnerability go hand in hand. Honesty is not just a matter of recounting the facts about ourselves. The feelings behind the facts also need to be shared. As we share honestly the different parts of ourselves, we become more exposed. At first, we don't know how the other person will respond. Honesty requires a willingness to take a risk, and see what will happen. If the other person responds insensitively – they ignore us, or start giving advice or making some judgement – we may feel slighted or hurt, and be reluctant to take further risks.

However, we will have gained a very valuable insight into their ability to respond, so risk taking of this nature is nearly always worthwhile. If their response is insensitive, we can share with them how it makes us feel. This gives them the opportunity to review their behaviour, and adjust it if they see fit.

If they are unable or unwilling to change, we have a clearer idea of where we stand with them, and what the limitations of the relationship are going to be. From this clarity we can decide if they are still the right person for us to share our lives with.

At other times the risk will pay off, and we find that when we make ourselves vulnerable our partner responds with acceptance, warmth and understanding. Our vulnerability in that moment makes us especially receptive to the warmth of their response, and our heart will open to them in a new and deeper way. If a few similar experiences happen with the same person, it gives us confidence in their ability to respond, and we will find that a loving intimacy develops of its own accord.

Vulnerability is not something that always needs to be shared verbally. It is, however, something that we need to cultivate within ourselves. We cultivate vulnerability by sharing with another, or admitting to ourselves, what is in our heart. Take for example the longing to be loved. If we are aware of this as a felt experience, we may not wish to admit it or expose it to our partner. It is a common experience to feel sensitive or protective about these very personal feelings. We may, instead, try to get our partner to love us without having to be vulnerable. We start dropping hints, holding secret expectations, or even making outright demands.

Often, however, this doesn't work. If we are not vulnerable, we will also not be receptive. Even if our partner *is* loving, we will not be able to let it in, and our hearts will remain un-nourished.

Before we can receive anything, we must open ourselves up, and we do this by being vulnerable. Sharing love means giving *and* receiving. Often we find it easier to give than to receive. As we get comfortable with being vulnerable, we can do both.

In describing these processes, I am using words to illustrate emotional exchanges that are to a large extent non-verbal. These suggestions are not to be taken as a prescription to be followed step by step. By grasping the spirit of what is being said, you can determine how best to apply it in your own life.

Trudi and John were both in their early forties, and had been together for fifteen years. Both were involved in successful careers, and held management positions in different companies. During our first session, they said they were increasingly becoming 'strangers'. He felt that regular sex helped to keep the relationship going, while she said she would prefer more sharing of inner feelings.

Externally, they had a 'perfect home, perfect jobs and perfect looking relationship'. They said they still loved each other, but were no longer sure how to express it. They both agreed that 'life looks full, but feels empty'.

It was clear that Trudi was experiencing more dissatisfaction than John. She was asked to express some of her feelings, while John was asked just to listen.

> TRUDI: I don't like it when you turn to me for sex most evenings.
> It makes me feel…..I don't know……like I'm just a body for you.
> JOHN: I think sex relieves the stresses of the day for both of us
> TRUDI: I don't want to be just your stress-buster. Why can't we have more sharing without sex?

> *Trudi's tone is angry, resentful.*
> *She is asked to tell John how she feels.*

> TRUDI: I am angry with you. I'm sorry I can't help it.
> JOHN: I didn't know you felt like that
> TRUDI: Well….I do.

> *Trudi is asked to tell John what she wants.*

> TRUDI: (sighing)……(silence)……..I don't know. I can't say.

The atmosphere is very charged. Both are asked just to be with their feelings, and express them when they are ready.

TRUDI: You used to be always happy to see me. I used to look forward to you coming home. You would say nice things to me how proud you were of me, how you liked what I had done. Now you just come home and sit in silence in front of the TV. I feel like I don't exist for you anymore.

Silence.

TRUDI (in tears): I just want to know if I still matter to you. If I don't, you can tell me. I just can't stand this nothingness anymore. I can't stand it. I'd rather leave you, if that's what you want.
JOHN: Of course you matter to me.
TRUDI: You never show it. How can you say 'Of course'. How am I supposed to know?

John is asked to express what he feels.

JOHN: I know that I care about you, but to be honest, my feelings are not much there anymore. I don't think it's because of you. When I come home, I'm tired. I don't want to talk. Sex makes me feel more close to you. I didn't know you were so unhappy about all this.

The first session ended there. There had been honesty on both sides, and Trudi had exposed her feelings and vulnerability. John had identified a lack of connection with his feelings.

John was asked to start paying more attention to his feelings. He expressed a willingness to do so.

In subsequent sessions, this turned out to be the main stumbling block. It became clear to both of them that they had grown apart, and were unable to find a way of re-connecting. Eventually, John asked for some private sessions to try to get through his part of the problem.

In counselling, John admitted to being afraid of letting go, and exposing the 'messy world' of his feelings. He recalled how being vulnerable had made him feel 'dependant' on Trudi in the past. He had been disturbed by this feeling, and had deliberately pulled away from it. It made him feel that he 'wasn't in control anymore', and that she had too much of a hold over him.

This was the core of the whole problem. John saw vulnerability as a sign of weakness and loss of control – and he was very uncomfortable with it.

Now he was also seeing that his lack of vulnerability had caused them to grow apart, and to feel like 'strangers'.

John was in a dilemma. To be (vulnerable), or not to be? He actually disliked both options.

One thing I seldom do with clients is rush them towards a solution. In my experience something more meaningful happens when you simply identify the issue or dilemma, and sit with it. There was no reason why John *should* become more vulnerable – the decision of which way to go had to come from him.

John was faced with one of the biggest challenges of his life. Whether to let go of the controls he had placed around the vulnerable side of his heart, and open up to loving someone?

The turning point for him came unexpectedly. I asked him at one point what it was that he appreciated about Trudi. He said, flippantly 'Well, she has put me in this dilemma!' Suddenly, the truth behind this statement dawned on him. It was the dilemma, and his struggle with it, that was the most meaningful thing in his life right then – and Trudi had been instrumental in creating it for him. Seeing this, he burst into tears. For the first time in many years, he realised how much she meant to him.

In that moment, he rediscovered his love for her – and his vulnerability.

John's dilemma is something that everybody has to face at some time or other. The difficulty for John had been the feeling of not being in control, and of being 'dependant'.

Equating vulnerability with dependence is a common fear. I believe it is a hang-over from childhood, when these two feelings usually existed in us together. As a child, you loved your mother – and you were dependant on her. In your mind, these two feelings become intertwined. As adults, we need to learn how to be vulnerable, open and loving with someone, while at the same time remaining centred and independent. The final sessions with John were about how to attain this balance.

The key to attaining this balance is to shift your focus from the beloved to the source of love inside your self. If your focus is too much on the beloved, you will start to identify them as the source of your love. You think you love them because of *them*. This makes you anxious, off-centre, attached and dependant on them. If you shift your focus to the source of love inside your self, you can love openly and abundantly without becoming attached or dependant. You recognise that you love someone, not just because of them, but mostly because of what is arising in *you*. You recognise yourself as the source of love.

5. Practice the Three A's

The three A's are the way in which we can best transform our negative emotional states. When we discover emotions such as anger, jealousy, possessiveness, fear, mistrust and so on, it is not helpful to ignore them, or try to make them go away. Neither is it helpful to give them free rein and let them control us. To deal with them effectively, we need to transform them, so that the energy behind them turns from a negative state into a positive one.

The three A's are *awareness, acceptance and affirmation*. When an emotion such as anger or jealousy arises in us, the first thing is to be aware of it. When we are not aware of it, we can start to rationalise and justify all sorts of controlling and demanding behaviours. We need to stop these behaviours and ask ourselves "What is the emotion that is driving them?" We then just feel what is happening in the body. We don't try to figure out or analyse what the emotion must be. The body will tell us what it is as a felt experience.

An example of this comes from a client I had recently. He had been involved in a relationship for the past two years, and he and his partner had been exploring ways of making their connection a

Tantric one. In the two months leading up to our sessions, his partner had begun to show an interest in another man. According to her,
it was an innocent friendship. Yet he was unhappy about it. He told
her that if she was 'going to put her energy out with other men', it
would disturb the Tantric connection they were developing, and he
would have to stop seeing her.

He felt quite justified in taking this stance. It seemed to him to be
a rational one. Yet when we started to explore the emotions underling
it, he finally admitted to feeling hurt and angry and insecure about her
friendship with this man. His threat and ultimatum to her was based
on an effort to control her, and to avoid feeling his own insecurity.
Far from being rational, his stance was very much emotionally based.
When he could see and accept this, the focus came back to dealing
with his own insecurity, rather than the ultimatum to his partner.

After becoming *aware* of the emotion, the next step is to *accept* it. Feel
the feeling, and just accept that in this moment you are angry or jealous
or whatever. Don't try to change it, or even wish that it was different.
Be with the negative emotion, and just experience it as a feeling in
your body. Get to know the feelings and thoughts of anger and jealousy. If the anger is strong, allow it to be released from your body.
You can do this by allowing yourself to fume inside, feeling the sensation of anger burning through you. At the same time, glare the
emotion out through your eyes. If you need to, release it physically by
hitting a cushion, stomping, shouting etc. By doing this, you will find
that after some time, the emotion will subside, and you will be free of it.

With the emotion no longer driving your thoughts and behaviour, you are ready to move on to the third step – *affirmation*. Make a
positive affirmation to change your old way of thinking. The following are some affirmations, which, if repeated, will counteract various
negative emotional states.

EMOTION	AFFIRMATION
Anger	I understand the other person. I feel compassion for him/her
Jealousy	I love myself. I am loveable. The universe is abundant, and always gives me what I need. I rejoice in other people's happiness
Possessiveness	I recognise and respect other people's freedom to follow their own destiny
Fear	I trust that life and the universe are always taking care of me (*see also Chapter 3)*
Mistrust, suspicion	I recognise that people are doing what they need to do. I see others' actions with eyes of goodwill and trust

6. Forgiveness

The practice of forgiveness is a powerful and immediate way of transforming ourselves. With forgiveness, something magic happens. All our tendencies towards anger, resentment, bitterness, revenge and feeling victimised are wiped out. Forgiveness raises us out of our base, reactive nature, and it ennobles us. Through forgiveness, we discover a quality of the heart that is god-like. With forgiveness, we rise above the petty considerations of who did what, and who owes who. With forgiveness, we are saying 'I am more than this body that you have mistreated. I am more than these possessions that you have dishonoured. You cannot touch the deepest part of my heart and spirit. In my heart there is forgiveness for you.'

Forgiveness frees us of anger and resentment, and opens up a flow of nectar in our hearts. It is very helpful to practise forgiveness for negative aspects of past relationships with parents and siblings. When we forgive, the negative feelings we have towards a person or situation are lifted from the heart. We forgive as much for our own benefit, as for the benefit of the relationship.

We can do the same thing in an intimate relationship, but with one difference. If our partner has wronged us in some way, they may apologise and ask for forgiveness. If their remorse is sincere, then it will be easy for us to forgive them. Sometimes, however, our partner may be unaware of the harm or hurt their behaviour has caused. Then we can ask for an apology before offering forgiveness. This will help bring awareness to their behaviour, and avoid the likelihood of it happening again. With small irritations, however, tolerance and acceptance and forgiveness can be something we practice for our own peace of mind.

Finally, when we recognise our own shortcomings, or when we have been neglectful or acted unconsciously towards others, we need to make amends with the other person, perhaps by offering an apology. We may also want to forgive ourselves for our failings. It saves a lot of self-castigation, and relieves the heart of its burden of guilt.

7. Gratitude

Cultivating an attitude of gratitude helps the heart to stay open. Its opposite, an attitude of complaint, just causes the heart to contract. Gratitude is what arises in us when we have no expectations. When we can accept and rejoice in whatever comes our way. It arises in a state of innocence, which is one of the most essential qualities of the heart.

If you are a "the-glass-is-half-empty" type of person, then cultivating gratitude will be helpful for you. There are so many things in life that we take for granted. The air that we breathe, our health, our community, our jobs, our freedom, our entertainment options, our friends, our family, our leisure time, our bodies, the food on the table, our education, pop-up toasters, well maintained roads, the security of our environment, birds, our ability to grow, the ocean, the kitchen sink, dancing, mobile phones, giving gifts, hot showers, books, favourite TV shows, the laughter of children, public transport, restaurants, the police service, a bowl of cherries, Tibetan bowls, teflon pans, pan flutes, washing machines, our ability to heal, the potential we have, a walk in the park.

I could go on – I haven't even mentioned lotuses or airplanes or spiritual teachers – but you get the idea. If you become aware, the glass is not half empty – it is overflowing. Gratitude is the heart's response to the divine for all we have been given. While our relationships with people are subject to change, our relationship with the divine remains constant. It is the one permanent, unchanging relationship we have. Gratitude is one way to cultivate this relationship.

Like all qualities of the heart, gratitude has a childlike innocence about it. It is unconditional. We don't bargain with the divine for a better deal. We humbly accept with gratitude all that is, while at the same time striving to make more of the divine perfection manifest here on earth – in our behaviour and in our environment.

As the Tao Te Ching says 'From the One comes Two, and from the Two come the ten thousand things'. Gratitude for the ten thousand things brings us closer to the One.

Summary

To open the heart, and to share love with another, there are things that are helpful, and things that are harmful. We can summarise them in the following table.

DO	DON'T
Be here and now	Try to create love
Be non-possessive	Avoid pain
Cultivate Trust	Project into the future
Be honest & vulnerable	Make demands and expectations
Practice the three A's	Be judgemental
Practice Forgiveness	Create attachment
Be Grateful	Control and manipulate

Chapter 7

The Dharma of Love

In the preceding chapters we have described the steps involved in creating a genuinely loving relationship with another person. These include:

- transforming the instinctual energies of sex and survival
- letting go of possessiveness
- giving up the desire for control &/or being more assertive
- becoming more honest and vulnerable
- giving up judgements
- staying in the present moment as much as possible

What has been presented in this book is a set of guidelines. These can be used to help you on your journey of transformation. For most people, transforming their old, unconscious habits and behaviour patterns into a new way of relating will take some time and effort. Just reading this book is unlikely to change your relationships. Old habits die hard. We all have some resistance to change. At first, the ideas in this book will affect only the conscious part of your mind. You will gain an intellectual understanding. Your sub-conscious thought patterns, and the behaviours they give rise to, will not be affected. And it is these thoughts and behaviours that have the most powerful influence over you. The conscious mind exists only on the surface – it consists of just 10-15% of the total mind. The sub-conscious and unconscious layers of the mind take up at least 85% of the total mind.

Your conscious mind may already be very enlightened. However, these are just the thoughts you have when you are sitting comfortably in your armchair. Your sub-conscious thoughts are the ones that come up on the bungy platform, or during some crisis point in your relationship. These are the moments that reveal your fears, selfishness, possessiveness and all the other unloving tendencies you carry in your sub-conscious. It is these thought patterns that you need to transform, and bring into harmony with the guidelines in this book.

This is not something that will happen overnight. It happens bit by bit. The nature of the unconscious is such that it is mostly hidden from us. We only discover the extent of our possessiveness, judgements and so on, over time. Each time you are honest with yourself, and recognise an old habit of possessiveness or judgement, and deliberately make an effort to give it up and replace it with an attitude that is loving, accepting and non-possessive – you take another step on the journey to love. At first things may seem to be moving slowly. Then one day you discover that many old habits have loosened their grip, and love comes more easily and spontaneously.

This transforming of old habits can only happen when you make a commitment to change. It won't happen just by wishing it to, or through intellectual understanding. A commitment involves the whole of your being – body, mind, heart and spirit. You have to really want to find love, and be prepared to do whatever it takes to make it a reality in your life. We have called this commitment the TIC (Transforming the Inner-self Commitment). Without a sincere commitment of this kind, your old habits and resistance to change will continue to control you – and love will remain no more than an elusive dream.

The commitment you are making is a commitment to understand the true nature of love, and to bring your thoughts and actions into harmony with this. For example, if the true nature of love is non-possessive, you will firstly satisfy yourself that this is so. Then you will start to honestly examine your own thoughts and feelings, and if you discover yourself being possessive, you will make a deliberate effort to give up this attitude, and replace it with an attitude of respect for the other person's freedom. Note that you do not start by adopting an attitude of non-possessiveness. Real transformation involves firstly a recognition, and acceptance, of *what is*. Having seen this, you may then decide to give it up. Only in this way does adopting a new attitude become helpful. The old program has to be deleted first, before a new one can be installed. Otherwise, your newly adopted attitude will just be a facade – an attempt at covering an unrecognised and ugly reality.

The process of transforming unconscious, unloving habits has been described in the previous chapters. When we reflect on these processes, we recognise that the arising of love is not a haphazard thing. It is not just a matter of serendipity, or meeting the right person. Love arises in accordance with certain universal laws. If we want to bring more love into our lives, we need to understand these laws, and start applying them in our lives.

Universal Law

The universe operates in accordance with certain laws. This happens on all levels of existence – physical, mental, emotional and spiritual. We are familiar with the laws that operate on the physical level – we know that when we jump up, the law of gravity will bring us back down. Other laws, including the laws of love, we are less familiar with.

A universal law is something that you have no control over. It controls you. We learn to respect the physical laws of the universe as young children. This happens through trial and error – we fall over a few times, get our fingers burnt, stuff ourselves with sweets – till we realise that these things are painful. A boiling kettle hurts. Indigestion hurts. So we learn to adjust. Don't touch that hot thing. Stop after a few cookies. Don't climb on the edge of that chair.

It is our body – and the feeling of pain – that gives us these messages. Our body acts as a feedback system for dealing with the world, educating us in the ways of the world.

While most of us have come to understand and respect the physical laws of the universe, the same cannot be said about the universal laws of love. We continue to get our hearts bruised, and completely misunderstand how this happens. We continue to suffer loneliness, yet fail to learn what works and what doesn't work in a relationship. We think we can be judgemental, demanding, dishonest, or just merrily project into the future – and that these things will have no impact on our love lives.

As in the physical world, the world of the heart is governed by certain universal laws. If we fail to understand and respect them, one thing is certain – we will continue to suffer.

Where many people get stuck is in how they interpret their suffering. You think your pain is caused by someone else. You blame your partner, or your parents, or the lack of 'decent' men/women available, and so on.

You fail to recognise how you have shut yourself off from love. You don't see that your suffering is telling you something about *yourself*. You keep touching the boiling kettle, and blaming someone else for the pain.

You need to be clear that love does not function according to your ideas and wishes. Love functions according to it's own reality. Judging or critising someone because they don't measure up to your ideal is touching the boiling kettle. Projecting into the future is touching the boiling kettle. These things shut you off from the reality of love in that moment. *This* is what causes you pain. Your judgements and expectations are the things that most hurt you. They violate one of the universal laws of love, and inevitably cause you to suffer.

Many of the great teachers of the past have spoken of universal law. Buddha called it Dharma. Lao Tzu called it Tao. Jesus referred to it as 'The Will of the Father'. These laws apply to everyone. You have not been exempted. There has not been a meeting of the Masters of the Universe at which they all agreed that "Regarding the Universal Laws of Love, we've decided that Bob from Wisconsin shall be exempt for the rest of his life. He can do whatever he likes, and he'll still have lots of love in his life."

This hasn't happened. So next time you get hurt, rather than blaming the other person, ask yourself 'What universal law of love have I not respected?' Approach the question with some humility. Recognise that you may have made a mistake, and be grateful to the other person for creating a situation from which you can learn.

In general terms, universal law applies to different areas of our lives – health, karma, manifestation and so on. In this book I have set out the universal laws that govern the arising of love. The principles and guidelines in this book are not just the result of some academic study at a university psychology department. They are much more profound than that. They represent the end result of twenty years of my own personal journey – a journey that has taken me to India, Bhutan, Nepal, USA, UK and Australia, and which has involved several significant relationships. Transforming the energies of the heart has been a personal and spiritual practice for me, and it has also been a part of my work as a counsellor, therapist and meditation teacher. I can say that I understand the universal laws of love in the same way that a child knows about a boiling kettle. What is written in this book has been verified many times in my own experience, and in the experience of the people I have worked with.

The universal laws of love will help us to align our thoughts and behaviours with the true nature of the heart. However, they are just one side of the story of the Dharma of love. When we speak of the Dharma of love, we are speaking of the whole truth of love. There are two sides to the heart, and our thoughts and behaviours will affect only one of these two sides. They affect what we might call the right hand side of the heart – the active side. There is another side of the heart – one which we have no control over. This we may call the left hand side of the heart – the spontaneous side of love. In the remainder of this chapter, I want to look at this left hand side of the heart, and at how we can bring about a balance and integration between the two sides.

Heart and Spontaneity

Love is not just a matter of technique – of adopting certain attitudes, following guidelines and so on. These things will create the climate in which love can blossom, but the bloom itself will always be something unfathomable and beyond our grasp.

The arising of love in the heart always happens spontaneously. It just happens – *je ne sais quoi*, as the French say. You see someone – and you fall in love. Who knows what combination of karmic and astrological factors, personality, chemistry and other elements have contributed to this happening. All we can say is – it just happened. This is the left hand, spontaneous side of love; the *'que sera sera'* side of the story.

The two sides of the heart correspond to the two colours that are normally associated with heart energy – pink and green. The left hand side is the feminine aspect, and is represented by the colour pink. Pink is also symbolic of the blending of red and white – i.e. the energies of sexual passion and spirituality meet here. The right hand active side is the masculine aspect, and is represented by the colour green. Green is symbolic of vitality, of new leaves emerging in springtime. It represents new life, and is the energy that keeps love ever-new, fresh and alive in the Now.

When it comes to loving relationships, people generally fall into two categories. There are those who believe in romance, meeting the 'right' person and letting the magic happen. If the magic doesn't happen, or if it fades away, then it could not have been the right person.

The second type believes that relationships have to be worked at. They believe in the right hand of love – the active side. They will do and say all the right things, follow the guidelines and generally 'try' to create a loving connection.

When we really understand the Dharma of love, we will see that neither of these approaches is complete. Each one represents only half of the story, and is not enough in itself to ensure a life of love. Love is magic – but it also needs an understanding of the laws of love to make it endure. Otherwise we can easily stifle the magic with our foolish behaviour. Love can cause you to soar up into the clouds – but you need two wings to fly. The left wing of spontaneity, and the right wing of acting in harmony with Dharma. Without this you'll be like a one-legged duck in a pond – just going round and round in circles.

To make love an on-going reality in your life – to make it last and endure – you need to balance and integrate the left hand and right hand sides of the heart. Balancing and integrating are two separate steps. Let's look at each one in turn.

1. Balancing Left and Right

The first step to balancing the left and right sides of the heart is to understand how these two sides are functioning in you at present. If the left side is more dominant, you will find yourself falling in love easily. The strong feelings you have will be difficult for you to express or share. When you are with someone, you find yourself shy and tongue-tied. Often the connection that you long for will fail to happen. If a relationship does develop, you will greatly enjoy the honeymoon phase, but then when difficulties start to arise, you will find yourself at a loss. You will either withdraw, or react very emotionally. You will feel that you have made a mistake, and have chosen the wrong person. If things deteriorate further, you will blame most of it on the other person, and look for some way to leave the relationship. When you are once more on your own, the cycle will repeat itself again.

If the right side is dominant, you will be more concerned with how you present yourself. Your focus will be on making a good impression on the other person. You will go to great lengths to arrange wonderful evenings, buy expensive gifts, make frequent phone calls and generally do all you can to impress the other person. You enjoy the thrill of the chase. If the other person plays hard to get, it makes you try even more. However, once you have won them over, then you quickly start to lose interest. By the time the honeymoon comes around, you are already bored, and looking for new territories to conquer. When difficulties arise, you revert to your attentive, charming and re-assuring ways. Yet your partner soon starts to sense that your heart isn't really in it, and that your attentiveness is just an act you are putting on. You know how to act in the right way, but your actions are motivated by a narcissistic ego rather than by genuine feeling. You want control and an enhanced self-image, rather than a relationship based on genuine love and intimacy.

To sum up, the left-side dominant person feels, but doesn't know how to act. The right-side dominant person can act, but does so without any feeling.

Before you can bring about a balance in yourself, you need to know where your imbalance lies. You need to recognise where you are still incomplete. Is your difficulty with taking action? Or is it that you act without feeling?

If your difficulty lies in taking action, then make a commitment to yourself that henceforth you will start acting on your feelings. Listen to what is arising in your heart – and summon up the courage to act on that in some appropriate way. Develop ways of communicating your feelings to others. Take a course in communication skills. Learn the subtleties of verbal and non-verbal communication. Become more assertive. Learn when assertiveness is appropriate, and when it isn't. Spend time listening to your heart. Understand how the feelings in your heart want to be expressed. What form of expression gives you the greatest joy? Is it music, or dance, or teaching or helping others? Try different things and see how they make you feel. Develop confidence in your intuition.

If your difficulty lies in knowing what you feel, then you need to slow down and get back in touch with yourself. Recognise that your actions are motivated by control and narcissism, and stop acting on these kinds of motives. Ask yourself 'Do I want a genuinely loving relationship?' If the answer is 'yes', then make a commitment to yourself that you will do all that is necessary to bring this about. If you have trouble experiencing your feelings, get some professional help. Go into therapy for a while. Otherwise, stop the game-playing and start being honest with yourself and others. Before taking any action, ask yourself 'How do I feel right now?', 'Do I really want to do this?', 'What is my motive for doing this?' Be honest with yourself. Let your actions flow from genuine heart-felt feelings.

There is another reason why we may have difficulty experiencing the left hand, spontaneous side of the heart. Rather than the right side being overly controlling, it may be that the left side of the heart has become blocked. This blocking of spontaneous feeling can occur as a result of a build-up of negative feelings – especially pain and resentment. These feelings can accumulate in the heart and get stuck there, acting like a log-jam that prevents any other feeling from flowing spontaneously. This happens through an actual physical contraction in the muscles surrounding the heart area. If this is the case, the old stuck feelings need to be released before the spontaneous side of the heart can open up again. We have discussed how pain can be released from the heart in the previous chapter.

These descriptions represent the extremes that this kind of imbalance can take. For most people, their imbalance will lie somewhere in-between. As the left and right sides of the heart start coming into balance, your relationships will develop a new joy and harmony. Love will arise more spontaneously in you, and you will appreciate each other's company more and more. Then some more subtle adjustments can be made – adjustments relating to the integration of the left and right sides. Eventually, the distinction between action and feeling goes, and the two sides will function together as a unified whole.

2. Integrating Left and Right

Now we come to one of the most essential and profound steps on the whole journey to love. The integration of the left and right sides of the heart – the spontaneous and the active – is not something you will find in much of the literature about loving relationships. Most books talk only about one or the other side of the story. The self-help books focus mostly on the right hand side – the active side. Known as 'How To' books, they are concerned with the dos and don'ts of relationships.

Then there are the books of poetry and personal stories, which focus mostly on the left hand side of the heart – the spontaneous side. Here we find descriptions of the dramas of relationships in all their aspects and seasons. We can share the author's highs and lows, and get some vicarious thrill from descriptions of love's splendour and pain.

Reading these different authors, one sometimes wonders if the two camps are aware of each other's existence. Do the 'How To' authors read poetry? Do the storytellers ever read self-help books? One gets the feeling that those in the poets and storytellers camp generally regard themselves as more profound than those in the 'How To' camp. Yet one finds that most stories of love are filled with large doses of pain and suffering, and a lot of ignorance of the nature of love.

It is rare to meet someone in whom these two aspects of the heart are balanced and integrated. Especially when it comes to integration, we are getting into somewhat unchartered territory. How does such a person operate? What kind of relationships would they have? There is not a lot of reference material around relating to these questions. Dostoyevsky wrote a book, *The Idiot*, in which he attempted to portray an essentially 'good' character, but the hero comes across as rather stilted and unworldly. We do find some clues in writings from the East – Jalaludin Rumi, Rabindranath Tagore, and Paramahansa Yoganada have all given beautiful descriptions of this state. However, the only way to really know it, dear reader, is to bring about this integration within yourself.

In this section, we will look at some ways in which you can do this.

As the two sides start coming together, then the life-long dance between them can get underway. This dance between the two is what makes us feel fully alive. Without it, we will miss most of the deeper joys and richness that life has to offer – to say nothing of the fulfilment of an intimate relationship.

The dance is something that is difficult to describe. It will take a different form with each person, depending on your individual character, preferences and soul's purpose. From my own experience, it is the left-hand, spontaneous side of the heart which takes the lead. You stay tuned in to your feelings as they arise spontaneously, and you use that to decide how to act. As much as possible, you allow your actions to also be spontaneous – and you continue to stay tuned to your feelings. You use your feelings as a monitor. They will tell you if the course of action you are taking is the right one, or not. For example, in a relationship, if your feelings start to fade with the other person – look at what adjustment you need to make in your thoughts or behaviour to bring the feeling back. Be aware that you cannot control your feelings directly. You can only control your thoughts and behaviours. The spontaneous arising of positive feeling – or lack of it – is a direct feedback from your heart as to whether your current thoughts and behaviours are in harmony with Dharma, or not.

By controlling and adjusting your thoughts and behaviour, note what effect this has on your feelings. If your feelings improve, you are on the right track. If they don't – some other adjustment is required.

When following this process, you need to clearly understand that the spontaneous side of your heart *knows what it is doing*. There is an innate knowing, wisdom and intuitive intelligence operating there. This knowing operates beyond the level of the conscious mind. It is the left side of the heart that tells you what it is that you love, and how loving you are.

So creating a loving relationship is not just about following the guidelines of some book, or acting in the 'right' way. Ultimately, it is about listening to, trusting in and honestly sharing the spontaneous side of your heart. And it is in developing the wisdom to know when some adjustment is required in your thoughts and behaviour – and when it isn't. Sometimes the feeling can fade because you are behaving insensitively. And sometimes it fades because you have fulfilled your time together. Only honest self-reflection and a connection to your intuition will reveal these things.

It requires a considerable amount of courage to follow your heart in this way. You are acknowledging that the heart contains a greater wisdom than your head. Your heart will lead you to that which you love, whereas your head will only lead you to that which you desire. Chasing desires is an endless pursuit of the trivial, the mundane and the unfulfilling. The Buddha has called it the root cause of all suffering. You can recognise this in your own life. When you find yourself chasing money, security, power and control, material comforts and possessions – how does it make you feel? What happens in your heart?

No poet has ever eulogised over the joys of wearing a Rolex watch, or having a 25 square metre en-suite bathroom. These are not the things you will look back on fondly as you are lying on your deathbed. On your deathbed, you will remember how much love you did – or didn't – share in your life.

In this book, we have talked a lot about the Dharma of love as it applies to the right hand side of the heart. Our focus has been on getting our thoughts and behaviours aligned with the true nature of each of the chakras. We have not spoken much about the left hand side of the heart – its spontaneous side. In the remainder of this chapter, I would like to look at this aspect a little more closely.

Heart Essence

I have been suggesting in this chapter that the left hand side of the heart contains a far greater wisdom than what we carry in our heads. The implication is that, when making a major decision in your life, you should be listening to your heart more than your head. Your head is useful in that it will sort out all the practical aspects of your decisions. But it is useless in helping with the actual decision itself. In other words, it can help you with all the plans for the wedding – but it can't help you decide who to marry. For this decision, you need to listen to your heart.

The same applies to other major decisions – choosing a job, having a child, choosing where to live.

Then when it comes to the day-to-day interactions of a relationship, the same holds true. It is only by staying in touch with the spontaneous side of the heart, and following it, that your relationship will remain fresh, new and alive. If you settle in to routine behaviours, things will soon become stale and uninteresting.

The commitment to being open from the heart we have called the TOC (True to Oneself Commitment). It is a commitment to the truth of what is in your heart. And a commitment to maintaining the aliveness of the left side of the heart. From this everything else will flow. If your love remains alive, then the caring, attentiveness, support, and all the other things that go with a loving relationship, will be willingly given. Your partner will not have to nag or beg or demand these things from you. Love will be a joy rather than a duty.

For many people, living their lives in this way will require a leap of faith – faith in the wisdom of the heart. Most of us fear giving up control over our lives. We get attached to certain things. We want the relationship to go in a certain direction – and subtly start steering it that way. Our desire for control and security makes us afraid to be spontaneous from the heart. We don't trust in the heart's innate wisdom. We think we know better.

Yet you will find that the more you try to hang on to or control a relationship, the more it turns into a dead thing. Your efforts to control just squeeze the life out of the relationship. Check this with your own situation right now. Ask yourself honestly – how much love is spontaneously arising in my heart these days?

This is the only way we can know if our quest for love is reaching fulfilment. There will be more love spontaneously arising in our hearts.

In essence, we eventually discover that it is in the spontaneity of love that its great mystery resides. When we allow love to take us over, we discover its splendour and endless fascination. In the end, love demands from us a kind of surrender. This surrender, when we enter it knowingly, is the sweetest experience possible in life. We discover that love is not something that we have – it is something that has us. When we are in the presence of love, we are in the presence of something far greater than ourselves.

Love is far grander, wiser and more powerful than we are. It cannot be reduced to a few words or gestures. Our thoughts and actions can support the arising of love – but they cannot cause it.

What causes love? Nothing. Love is not caused by anything we do or say. Love is our essential nature. It is already there, waiting deep in our hearts for us to give up trying to control our lives, and surrender to it. Love demands from us a surrender – and then it rewards us with the greatest fulfilment in life. It gives us a seat at the table of the Gods, where we can drink a glass of their nectar with them.

Love connects us to our divinity. It is the bridge between heaven and earth. Love lifts us out of the mundane world, and allows us to soar in freedom, high above all of our petty problems. Love is the doorway to the divine, and the practice of aligning your thoughts and actions with Dharma removes the rust that has collected at its hinges. The door then swings open, and ushers you into the palace of the Gods. In the palace, a life of magnificence awaits you.

When the heart chakra awakens to its full potential – when our actions are in harmony with our feelings – there is a peace and tranquillity that arises in us, beyond anything we have previously known.

We started this book with a question – What is Love? The question became a quest – to find love, and to know it through experience. As the quest approaches its fulfilment, we are no nearer to answering the question. We still cannot say what love is. Love remains a mystery, but by participating in the mystery we see our question dissolve. Living and celebrating the mystery of love, we recognise its true nature.

In the end, love is beyond words. In stillness, in silence, its ineffable beauty and radiance are revealed to us. As the Sufi mystic, Rumi, puts it

What passed between us
in that luminous night
can never be written or told
On my final journey
from this world
the creases of my shroud
will reveal our story

Afterword

As you align yourself with your true nature at each of the first four chakras, your life and relationships will take on a new and different quality. Gone will be any sense of insecurity and uncertainty you have had about yourself. You will gain a much better understanding of who you are at these levels. Your ability as a lover will be greatly improved. Your old lack of confidence will give way to a growing, positive self-esteem. That gnawing sense of 'something missing' will be replaced by a feeling of being fulfilled at the heart.

As your self-esteem takes on a new, healthy, radiant glow, the possibility arises that it may even become a little *too* healthy. When we discover some essential truths about life that are not common knowledge, we may at first get a little carried away with ourselves. Some sort of messianic wish to save the planet – or at least the neighbourhood – may arise in us. Healthy self-esteem can turn into an inflated sense of our own importance.

I'm not suggesting we shouldn't reach out and help others. However, our motivation for doing so should be kept under scrutiny.

The issue of inflated self-esteem – another word for ego – will be dealt with in the second volume of this series on the chakras.

So this present volume is about turning a low self-esteem into a healthy one. The next volume will be about dealing with the inevitable ego issues that arise along with a healthy self-esteem. We will explore all the antics and disguises of the ego, and look at how to keep it in its place. We will see that spiritual growth is not about getting rid of the ego, but simply about becoming *disidentified* with it.

As we start to disidentify with the ego, the question of our

real identity will arise. If I am not who I think I am, then who am I
– really?

In the next volume in this series, we will approach the question
of ego and identity in a new and original way. We will explore how
to awaken the energies of the three highest chakras. This awakening
will lead to a direct recognition – beyond intellectual understanding
– of who we are.

Meanwhile, understanding and aligning yourself with the true
nature of the first four chakras will give you countless hours of joy,
amusement, bliss and challenge – and may be considered a preparation for entering into the deeper exploration of the higher chakras.

For information on courses, purchases and reviews relating to
this book, or to share your personal reviews and stories, visit our
website at:
www.awaken-love.com
or email us at
info@awaken-love.com

Visit Frank Vilaasa's blog at:
http://whatislovebyfrankvilaasa.wordpress.com/